D0992009

The
VOYAGE
of the
HUNLEY

The
VOYAGE
of the
HUNLEY

EDWIN P. HOYT

BURFORD BOOKS

Printed in the United States of America

10   9   8   7   6   5   4   3   2   1

Library of Congress Cataloging-in-Publication Data
Hoyt, Edwin Palmer.
    The voyage of the Hunley / Edwin P. Hoyt.
        p.   cm.
    Includes index.
    ISBN 1-58080-094-7 (hardcover)
    1. H. L. Hunley (Submarine).   2. United States—History—
Civil War, 1861–1865—Naval operations—Submarine.
    3. Submarines (Ships)—United States—History—19th century.
    4. Confederate States of America. Navy—History.   I. Title.
E599.H4 H69   2002
973.7'57—dc21   2002151505

CONTENTS

PREFACE

THE SAGA OF THE Confederate submarine *H. L. Hunley* is one of the true highlights of naval warfare and is unsurpassed for its dramatic impact. The three crews of the *Hunley* were heroes all and they have been so honored in the annals of the Confederacy. More, since the story has become known people from all across the world have traveled to Charleston to view the tiny submarine and hear its tale.

At the moment of this writing there remain several mysteries about the *Hunley* and one controversy. Three of the mysteries are: Why did the submarine sink? Why did the crew die? And why was the boat built with ballast tanks open to the crew compartment?

The answers to the first two questions may lie in the third. Given the engineers' knowledge of their subject, it would seem to have been sensible to enclose the ballast tanks, which could be purposefully flooded or emptied to submerge or surface the vessel, thus preventing accidental flooding of the submarine. The *Hunley*'s own experience dictated such a course: an accidental sinking in Charleston Harbor in 1863 and the loss of five men of the crew drowned occurred when the boat flooded after hatches were left open and the diving fin mechanism was accidentally depressed. The deficiency could then have been corrected, but was not.

The controversy concerns the discovery of the *Hunley*'s resting place in Charleston's outer harbor more than a century after the sinking.

Explorer Edward Lee Spence, underwater archaeologist Mark Newell, and author Clive Cussler have all at one time claimed to have discovered the *Hunley,* or believed they knew where it sank. Cussler's claim rests on the activities of his NUMA diving team. Newell's claim rests on his study of the *Hunley* over many years and his intuitive feeling that it lay in Maffitt's Channel because that was the logical place for it to be. Spence's claim rests on good luck; he says he found the *Hunley* one day in 1970 quite by accident when on a fishing trip.

At the moment Cussler's claim is paramount, accepted officially by the Hunley Commission.

The matter has now gotten into federal litigation. It should never have gone so far. Newell has abandoned his claim. Spence continues to press his case, insistent (and this author agrees with him) that he first found the

Hunley. Cussler should rectify his claim to cover only the "rediscovery" of the submarine, and the technical proofs that led to its identification as the *Hunley.* There exists plenty of glory for all.

—EDWIN P. HOYT
Tokyo 2002

1

THE SUBMARINE
IN WARFARE

EVER SINCE CIVILIZED MAN began his endless tussle with the sea, some have dreamed of conquering the depths of Neptune by sailing beneath the waves. Alexander the Great was supposed to have descended to the bottom of the sea in a watertight chamber. When he was laying siege to the Phoenician city of Tyre, Phoenician divers swam out under water to destroy the huge stone jetties his engineers had built to block the harbor. In the 16th century, when the Turks laid siege to the island of Malta, the Christian knights who ruled the island used divers to build an underwater barricade across the Grand Harbor.

The idea of the submarine was explored by Leonardo da Vinci, who drew plans for a submarine along with those of aircraft and other engineering marvels. Scores of others followed with their dreams, but they remained dreams until people began to understand engineering principles. Early attempts to build submersible craft uniformly ended in failure, usually drowning those who manned them. Secrets of water pressure, propulsion, and lighting had to be learned. The first submarines used candles for lights, which ate up oxygen quickly. But by the time of the American Revolution many of these things had been learned. A young graduate of Yale College named David Bushnell invented the first successful submersible, named the Turtle, which was used to try to sink a British man-of-war in New York Harbor. An American army sergeant named Ezra Lee volunteered to use the egg-shaped craft against the British fleet, and one dark night in 1776 the Turtle was brought down from its birthplace in New Rochelle to the Hudson River. On the outgoing tide two rowboats carried it out into the water of the harbor; Sergeant Lee boarded, closed the hatch, and submerged. He carried a mine of gunpowder destined for the bottom of one of the wooden warships, anchored near Governor's Island, off the tip of Manhattan.

The charge was set to explode in several hours. Sergeant Lee was to screw it into the bottom of the man-of-war HMS *Eagle,* a 64-gun ship. But when he tried to attach the mine, the screw would not penetrate the copper bottom of the warship, although he tried in several places. Near daybreak Sergeant Lee gave up, cast loose the mine, and made his way back to the American shore, never knowing the reason for his failure.

Although the Turtle never did succeed in sinking a ship, it came to the attention of inventor Robert Fulton. Fulton developed a mine that could be towed to attach to a warship and also a submarine to tow the mine. He offered these ideas to Napoleon's navy. In May 1801 Fulton and a French sailor made the first trial run of the 21-foot-long iron and copper boat, called the *Nautilus,* in the Seine River, which runs through Paris. They remained under water for 20 minutes. Later that year, Fulton perfected his submarine and demonstrated its effectiveness by towing a mine against the side of a warship and sinking it. He offered to build submarines for the French government to use against England, but the French turned him down on moral grounds. "The submarine is an immoral weapon," said French minister of marine Pleville le Pelle.

Fulton then crossed the English Channel and offered his services to the English, but they also turned him down on moral grounds. "Fiendish weapons," the British admirals called the submarines.

Fulton then returned to the United States, where he got an advance of $5000 to develop a submarine. But in the end the Americans rejected the submarine, too. People wanted steamboats, not submarines, said the U.S. admirals. So reluctantly Fulton put aside his plans for submarines, and spent the rest of his life building steamboats.

Still, the submarine idea lived on in America, and during the War of 1812 a Fulton-built submarine attacked the British warship *Ramillies* off the Connecticut coast, raising a storm of protest on both sides of the Atlantic against this "inhuman" weapon.

It was not until the American Civil War, as inhuman a struggle as ever existed, that the submarine came into its own. And the laurels, such as they were, for being first to sink an enemy warship were to go to the Confederacy, which produced the submarine CSS *Hunley*.

2

THE HUNLEY

HORACE L. HUNLEY, the principal backer of the submarine that would bear his name, was born into a wealthy sugar-planting family of Sumner County, Tennessee, on December 29, 1823, but spent most his life in New Orleans. He was educated at Tulane University, and studied law. As a lawyer and planter he became a fiery advocate of southern rights and was quick to join the Confederate cause when the states began seceding from the Union in 1860. He was already a Louisiana state legislator and had been given the political reward of the deputy collectorship of customs at New Orleans. In his late thirties, physically he was a handsome man with a broad forehead; dark eyes, hair, mustache, and beard; and a triangular chin.

In June 1861 Hunley led an expedition to Cuba to discover trade routes through which munitions could be shipped to New Orleans. The mission was successful but short lived, for soon Admiral David Farragut captured New Orleans. By that time Hunley was already deeply involved in the making of a submarine. He had joined with his brother-in-law Robert R. Barrow, lawyer and newspaper editor H. J. Leovy, and James K. Scott to bankroll a submarine venture begun by inventors James R. McClintock and Baxter Watson, proprietors of a machine shop on the New Orleans harborfront. Before the war began McClintock had been a riverboat captain on the Mississippi River. The work, secretly carried out in the machine shop at 31 Front Levee and at the Leeds Foundry nearby, would produce a Confederate submarine, launched early in 1862 and christened *Pioneer*.

The *Pioneer* was a cigar-shaped craft, built of quarter-inch steel plate bolted to an iron frame. "An oversized cigar" its inventors called it fondly, painted black, without superstructure, entry gained by the four-man crew through an 18-inch hatchway amidship. There was no pilothouse, only a pair of glass-covered portholes to assist navigation. In semidarkness the crewmen sat on U-shaped brackets bolted to the deck turning a crank attached to the propeller. The only light was provided by candles. When the vessel was only partially submerged, fresh air could be introduced by a rubber hose. This primitive *schnorkel* came to the surface supported by a wooden float; a stopcock inside the hose kept water from flowing in once the craft was completely submerged.

The *Pioneer,* however, was not destined to be the first Confederate submarine to attack the enemy. That distinction was held by designer William Cheeney's boat, manufactured at the Tredegar Iron Works in Richmond. In the fall of the year 1861 the Cheeney boat, manned by three

H. L. Hunley, in a photograph from 1860. Courtesy Louisiana State Museum.

James R. McClintock. Courtesy Naval Historical Center.

men, attacked the USS *Minnesota,* flagship of the North Atlantic Blockading Squadron, commanded by Flag Officer Louis M. Goldsborough. The attack occurred in the James River in Virginia. Two men of the crew operated the hand crank that powered the vessel. The third man, in diving gear, was stationed at the bow of the vessel, in a special lookout chamber. A floating camouflaged hose provided air to all three of the crew. When the target ship came within view the third man exited the submarine and tried to attach an explosive device to the bottom of the *Minnesota*. But the submarine was caught in the grappling that hung from the ship's jib boom. When the submarine crew thought they were underneath the hull they tried to screw the torpedo into the ship's bilge, and came near losing the boat and their lives as a result. They managed to escape without damaging the *Minnesota,* but Goldsborough ordered the area dragged for the breathing hose; it was picked up by a Union ship at the mouth of the James. A story and illustration of the "infernal machine" appeared in the November 1861 issue of *Harper's Weekly.*

By that time the Union was also deeply involved in the production of a submarine. In May that year the Philadelphia newspapers reported on the capture by Union navy officers of a strange vessel on the Delaware River. It was the creation of French inventor Brutus de Villeroi, a submarine thirty-three feet long and four feet in diameter, which had reportedly submerged and remained under water for three hours, propelled by a crank, steered by rods connected with movable outside fins, complete with pumps, brass faucets, and pigs of lead for ballast. In November the Union navy signed a contract for $14,000 with de Villeroi to build a larger version of the submarine. It was under construction at Martin Thomas's boatyard in Philadelphia, and was aimed to destroy the ironclad ship *Virginia* that the Confederates were building at Richmond. When completed it was christened the *Alligator* and propelled by a crank mechanism attached to a screw propeller.

The Confederate *Pioneer* was launched in New Orleans in February 1862 and taken to the navy yard at Government Basin for tests. These were conducted by backer James K. Scott, and were pronounced successful, although there were problems with the steering because of poor visibility under water. The boat was steered by a compass, which was unreliable, and so very often the submarine had to surface while the skipper took his bearings.

"This boat demonstrated to us the fact that we could construct a boat that would move in any direction and at any distance from the surface...." McClintock wrote after the trials.

The *Pioneer* was moved to Lake Pontchartrain for more tests. One March day she was tested for her ability to attack, and succeeded in blowing up a wooden barge moored in the middle of the lake. The floating torpedo explosive used in the attack was towed some distance behind the *Pioneer*. The sub would submerge and drag the torpedo into the barge, where it would explode on contact. Observers said that Skipper Scott took a careful reading of his position, then ordered the ballast tanks blown, and the submarine went down. Then came a silence so long that the observers fretted lest the *Pioneer* had been lost. Suddenly the waters of Lake Pontchartrain were upset by a tremendous explosion, which "blew the barge so high," wrote observer Thomas Scharf, "that only a few splinters were heard from."

McClintock said that the *Pioneer* then successfully attacked a number of other objects, including a schooner. The backers were so pleased that they applied for a letter of marque, which would give Confederate government authorization to sink enemy commerce. The letter was granted March 31, but Skipper Scott never had a chance to employ it. In April, New Orleans was attacked by Admiral Farragut's Union fleet and captured before the end of the month. The *Pioneer* was scuttled in the New Basin Canal, and the inventors and their backers hurriedly gathered their plans and moved to Mobile. The *Pioneer* was recovered by Union engineers and lay on the bank of the New Canal until 1868 when it was sold off for $43 for scrap.

When the *Pioneer* group reached Mobile, Horace Hunley plunged into the gay social swim and political life of the community while McClintock and Watson sought a suitable location to continue their work on a submarine. They found it in the Park & Lyons Machine Shop at the corner of Water and State Streets, a big building with a foundry, large cranes, and all else that they needed. Here they set to work to create *Pioneer II*. Meanwhile Horace Hunley made the acquaintance of Admiral Franklin Buchanan, the chief officer of Mobile's defenses. He found Admiral Buchanan receptive to anything that promised to break the federal blockade, but extremely skeptical of their chances of success with the submarine.

Hunley financed the entire venture, putting up $10,000. They were fortunate to meet Lt William A. Alexander, a bright young engineer assigned to temporary duty in the shop. He was an Englishman who had enlisted in the 21st Alabama Infantry Regiment. He worked closely with McClintock and Watson through the summer and autumn of 1862, experimenting with methods of propulsion, including an electromagnetic engine, but ultimately returning to the hand-cranked propeller.

Christened the *American Diver,* their finished submarine measured 36 feet in length, three feet in width, and was four feet high, tapered at both ends, with diving fins on either side of the bow. The new version had two hatchways instead of one, making it easier for the five or six men of the crew to get in and out. The new version also had a crude mercury gauge to determine depth as well as a compass.

Admiral Buchanan watched the submarine's trial runs and was dismayed to see how slowly the boat operated. He was also skeptical about the submarine's ability to deliver a payload against targets that sometimes lay as far as six miles offshore. By diving under a ship and exploding a torpedo against the enemy, "I don't think it could be effective against the enemy off the harbor," he said.

One day in February 1863 the inventors decided the submarine was ready for action and began to tow it to Fort Morgan, where it would be armed with a torpedo and fully manned to set out to sink an enemy ship. But the weather was rough, the seas high, and the submarine filled with water and finally rolled over and plunged to the bottom of Mobile Bay, where it rests to this day. Fortunately no lives were lost.

The building that housed the Park & Lyons Machine Shop in Mobile, Alabama—the birthplace of the Hunley—*in a photo from the early 1960s.* Courtesy Naval Historical Center.

Musing on the failure, Admiral Buchanan was caustic: "I told you so" he said. "I never entertained but one opinion as to the result of this boat—that it should prove a failure and such has been the case."

Horace Hunley and his inventors were sorely disappointed at the failure, but not dismayed. As McClintock later said, they knew the principles involved, and it was simply a question of proper application. They set to work immediately on a new boat. Admiral Buchanan had proved to be a false friend. Hunley turned now to General Dabney Herndon Maury, appointed military commander of the District of the Gulf. General Maury had the distinction of knowing something about underwater explosives; his uncle was Matthew Fountaine Maury, an underwater-explosives expert.

In the middle of 1863 Hunley joined with gunsmith E. C. Singer, who invested $5000; Hunley put up another $5000; and a further one-third interest want to a consortium of three men in Mobile: B. Gus Whitney, R. W. Dunn, and J. D. Breamer. Work continued at the Park & Lyons Machine Shop. The team was joined at this point by a friend of Lt. Alexander's, Army Lt. George Dixon, C.S.A.

The new boat was called "Whitney's submarine boat" after Gus Whitney; other names for it were the "Porpoise" and the "Fish Boat." This was the craft that ultimately came to be called the *Hunley*. It was fashioned from a

William A. Alexander. Courtesy Museum of Mobile.

boiler, probably from a steamer, 48 inches in diameter and 25 feet long, cut in two longitudinally, with 12 inch iron boiler strips inserted in her sides and lengthened by tapering to be thirty feet long, four feet wide, and not quite five feet deep.

Submarines dive and surface by ballast tanks, which are flooded with seawater to make the boat submerge, and pumped free of water to make it surface. The "Fish Boat" (aka *Hunley*) did the same. At each end of the boat were bulkheads, or walls, which formed water ballast tanks. Ballast was also provided by flat castings or keel ballast, which were fastened to the outside bottom of the shell by T-bolts that passed through watertight stuffing boxes in the interior. These T-bolts could be released if additional ballasts had to be jettisoned in order to allow the sub to surface. Each water tank had a seacock, which provided seawater for sinking and a pump for rising. A mercury gauge, open to the sea, indicated the depth of the boat. A one-and-a-quarter-inch shaft passed through stuffing boxes on each side of the boat, just forward of the end of the propeller shaft. On each end of this shaft, outside the boat, were secured fins five feet long and eight inches wide. Raising or lowering the ends of these fins changed the direction the boat would travel, either up or down.

The captain sat forward and operated the rudder by a wheel, connected to levers and rods. An adjusted compass was placed in front of the forward tank. The boat had an ordinary propeller, protected against fouling by an iron ring connected to the shaft; motive power was supplied by eight crewmen, sitting on the port side, turning cranks that formed a section of the propeller shafts.

It was no place for someone who suffered from claustrophobia—fear of close quarters. When the men were in place it was virtually impossible to pass fore and aft. The men reached their positions by passing through the fore and after hatchways, 12 inches by sixteen inches—automatically excluding the fat. The hatches had eight-inch

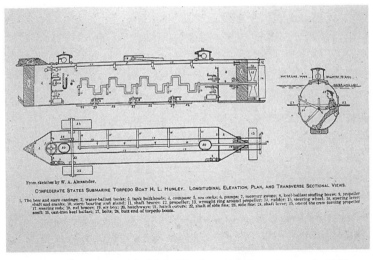

From sketches by W. A. Alexander.

CONFEDERATE STATES SUBMARINE TORPEDO BOAT H. L. HUNLEY. LONGITUDINAL ELEVATION, PLAN, AND TRANSVERSE SECTIONAL VIEWS.

1, The bow and stern castings; 2, water-ballast tanks; 3, tank bulkheads; 4, compass; 5, sea cocks; 6, pumps; 7, mercury gauge; 8, keel-ballast stuffing boxes; 9, propeller shaft and cranks; 10, stern-bearing and gland; 11, shaft braces; 12, propeller; 13, wrought ring around propeller; 14, rudder; 15, steering wheel; 16, steering lever; 17, steering rods; 18, rod braces; 19, air box; 20, hatchways; 21, hatch covers; 22, shaft of side fins; 23, side fins; 24, shaft lever; 25, one of the crew turning propeller shaft; 26, cast-iron keel ballast; 27, bolts; 28, butt end of torpedo boom.

W. A. Alexander's sketch of the H. L. Hunley, *made from memory in 1902.*

coamings with rubber gaskets, and hinged covers that fastened from the inside. In the coamings were glasses to sight from—the coamings were a sort of conning tower for the commander of the boat.

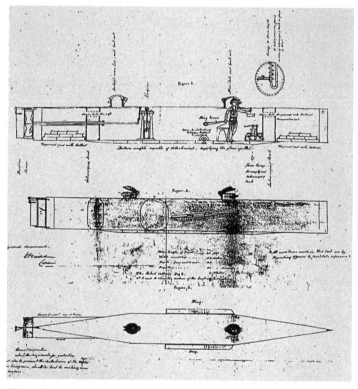

The earliest-known drawings of the American Diver *and the* Hunley, *made by James McClintock and given to the British navy in 1872.* Courtesy British Admiralty Records Division, researched by Mark Ragan and Richard Wills.

In the top of the boat was an opening for an air box, a hollow shaft with a stopcock on the outside to admit air but keep water out.

Here was a typical training exercise:

All hands aboard, they would fasten the hatches down tight, light a candle, then let the sea into the ballast tanks until the top of the shell was three inches under water. This could be ascertained by the water level showing through the glasses in the hatch coamings. The seacocks

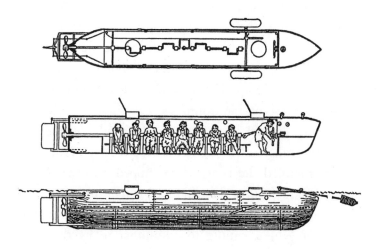

A sketch of the H. L. Hunley *made by Simon Lake from a description of the vessel by Charles Hasker, one of the crew who survived the first sinking.* Published in *McClure's* magazine in January 1899. Researched by Mark Ragan.

were then closed, the crew began turning the cranks, and the submarine got under way.

The captain then lowered the lever and depressed the forward ends of the fins, watching the mercury gauge for depth. When he leveled off the fins, the boat would level off, too. He could raise or lower the boat by manipulating the fins.

When they wanted to surface, if the boat was not moving, they had to start the pumps to lighten the load by pumping out seawater. When they made a landing the second in command would open the rear hatch cover, climb out, and pass a line to the shore.

Usually on these exercises McClintock was in command, although sometimes Hunley took a hand and sometimes Lt. George Dixon commanded. Whitney usually served as second in command.

On July 1, 1863, the submarine carried out a mock attack on a moored flatboat in the Mobile River. Nine volunteers manned the boat as she slipped into the water, dragging a torpedo at the end of a 200 foot line. The captain took a last compass reading, depressed the diving planes, and lit a candle for illumination as the boat dropped 20 feet below the surface and leveled off.

The submarine passed under the flatboat, the torpedo exploded, the submarine surfaced, and the men came out of the hatches accompanied by cheers and applause.

In the crowd was Admiral Buchanan, now a converted believer in the submarine. The next day he wrote Captain John Tucker, chief of the naval defenses of Charleston:

> Yesterday I witnessed the destruction of a lighter in the Mobile River, by a torpedo which was placed under it, by a submarine iron boat, the invention of Messrs Whitney and McClintock.
>
> Messrs Watson and Whitney visit Charleston for the purpose of consulting General Beauregard and yourself to ascertain whether you will try it, and they explain all its advantages, and it can operate in smooth water where the current is not so strong as was the case yesterday. Can recommend it to your favorable consideration, it can be propelled at about four knots per hour, to judge from the experiment yesterday I am satisfied it can be used successfully in blowing up one or more of the enemy ironclads in your harbor. Do me the favor of showing this to General Beauregard with my regards.

Captain Tucker did show the letter to General Beauregard, who became quite excited and called for an interview with Watson and Whitney. After looking over their drawings and listening to their plans he sent for the submarine.

On August 7 Beauregard telegraphed the railroad authorities, "Please expedite transportation of Whitney's submarine boat from Mobile here. It is much needed."

THE *HUNLEY* MOVES TO CHARLESTON

The *Hunley* was needed in Charleston, for this was the center of maritime activity in the Confederacy, particularly now that New Orleans was gone. It was also the center of the Union's effort to blockade and starve out the South. Admiral Dahlgren's Atlantic Blockading Squadron was based here, and conversely it was the central point for blockade runners.

Since colonial days Charleston had occupied the forefront of southern maritime life as well as southern social activity. Its mansions, gardens, and entertainments rivaled those of any in the New World, its ladies were the most stylish, its gentlemen the most civilized, its ambience the most international.

Charleston was the site of the failed Democratic Party convention of 1860. The southern Democrats had walked out of the convention and later met at Richmond. The Charleston convention adjourned after 57 ballots, and the northern Democrats met later at Baltimore and fielded a candidate for president. This split in the Democratic ranks led to the election of Abraham Lincoln on the Republican ticket. Those southerners who were hellbent on secession welcomed the victory of the Republicans, because it made secession inevitable.

Sentiment for secession was overwhelming, but there were a few stalwarts who advocated sticking with the Union. Such was Benjamin Franklin Perry, who refused to quit the convention. When the Ordinance of Secession was passed he told the delegation, "You are now going to the Devil and I will go with you. Honor and patriotism require me to stand by my state." Another was James Louis Pettigru, a leader of the Unionists in Charleston. The convention was assembled at the Baptist church. A stranger asked Pettigru where the insane asylum was located. He pointed at the Baptist church. "It looks like a church," he said, "but it is now a lunatic asylum. Go there and you will find 164 maniacs within."

On November 7, when the news reached Charleston that Lincoln had been elected, federal judge Magrath left his courtroom on Chalmers Street, locked the door, and walked home.

"Justice is dead," he said, "and the Temple of Justice is closed."

On December 17 the South Carolina Legislature met at Institute Hall in Charleston. Before the week was out the delegates had enacted the resolution of secession and declared South Carolina's independence. The streets were crowded with people, many of them wearing palmetto cockades or secession bonnets, shouting for secession. When the measure was enacted, the assembly went wild with excitement. Members leaped to their feet; in the street the crowd took up the shouting, cannon boomed, and the bells of St. Michael's Church rang out. The *Charleston Mercury* had an extra on the street within fifteen minutes, up went the palmetto flag, saluted by the

artillery, tar barrels blazed, and secession leaders were ser-
enaded. Next day the *Charleston Courier* editorialized,

> Thursday was a day destined to become famous in
> the annals of history. After long years of suffering
> and forbearance, the people of South Carolina have
> now thrown off the yoke of an odious and infamous
> union. We now stand before the world a disen-
> thralled and regenerated people, a glorious example
> of the brave and the free. The chains that have so
> long oppressed us have been thrown off the limbs
> they have shackled and consigned by patriots and the
> sons of Revolutionaries to dust. . . .

The same issue of the paper described the celebration of
the previous night: "One brilliant and prominent feature
was the cheerful and beautiful light which illuminated the
Secession Pole at the corner of Hayne and Meeting
streets." At first everything seemed to be favorable for the
new republic, founded on the principle of states' rights
and slavery. Vice President Stephens called slavery "the
cornerstone of the new edifice."

A problem arose: how to deal with takeover of the federal forts and arsenals in the seceding states. The plan was
to occupy them and pay later. What would the rest of the
states say about secession? The general belief was that
secession was the right of every state. This was reinforced
by a belief that the North would do nothing—"hasn't the
guts to fight."

General Beauregard. Courtesy National Archives.

This thesis was disproved in a hurry. After Fort Sumter fell to Confederate guns, President Lincoln called for volunteers to put down what he called an illegal rebellion.

An immediate sense of shock in the North was displaced by determination that "the erring sisters" must be brought back within the fold.

Equally strong in the South was the reaction to Lincoln's call for 75,000 volunteers The states that had originally rejected secession—Virginia, Arkansas, Tennessee, and North Carolina—now joined their sister southern states in secession. The war changed overnight from a conflict over states' rights to a regional struggle.

In the North the war was always known as the Rebellion. In the South it was first called the War for Independence, but as the struggle went on it became known as the War Between the States.

From the outset Charleston played a major role in the war. Union authorities were eager to capture Charleston because it was a base for blockade running. Small vessels darted out of Charleston Harbor, bound for Nassau with bales of cotton, returning with precious rifles, uniforms, and equipment for the Confederate army.

To check this blockade running, one of the first Union efforts was to block up the ports with sunken ships. In November 1861 a fleet of 24 old whalers sailed out of New Bedford, carrying in their holds 7500 tons of stones

Admiral Dahlgren. Mathew Brady photograph, courtesy National Archives.

gathered from New England farms. The fleet was manned by officers and men from Nantucket and New Bedford, led by Captain Rodney French, the mayor of New Bedford. A second fleet sailed in December under navy auspices. Sixteen of these ships were sent to Charleston and sunk off the bar in the channel to create "an impenetrable barrier." But the scheme fell flat, for it was not impenetrable, as many a blockade runner could testify in the next four years.

The Union, however, was unremitting in its attempts to block off Charleston port. At first the navy could put

Floating torpedoes on the dock at Charleston, ca. 1863. National Archives, courtesy Richard Mroczynski.

only 35 vessels in action, only three of them modern steam propelled. It was not until the spring of 1863 that the Union navy could bring up enough naval power to attack the Charleston forts. On April 2 that year Rear Admiral Samuel F. DuPont brought a fleet, including several iron-clad ships of the *Monitor* class, to attack Fort Sumter. Thereafter the blockade was maintained by this squadron. Admiral DuPont failed in his first attempt to capture Fort Sumter and was relieved by Admiral Dahlgren. Thereafter many attacks were made on the Charleston defenses, none of them successful for more

Street scene, Charleston, at harborside, ca. 1863. National Archives, courtesy Richard Mroczynski.

than a brief period. Key to the Charleston defense was Fort Wagner on Morris Island. Many attempts were made to storm that fort, but its defenders held out stubbornly.

Still, Charleston was ringed by Union ships, and blockade running was never easy. Small wonder then that General Beauregard was eager to have the services of the new submarine, which gave promise of breaking the Union blockade.

Abandoned "David" submersible in Charleston at the end of the war. Precursors to the Hunley, *"Davids" harassed blockaders in Charleston Harbor.* National Archives, courtesy Richard Mroczynski.

THE EARLY VOYAGES
OF THE *HUNLEY*

ON AUGUST 12 the submarine arrived in Charleston cradled on two flatcars. It was unloaded at the railroad station and then moved to the dock on the Cooper River. Hundreds of onlookers cheered as the boat rolled through Charleston's streets. General Beauregard ordered his quartermaster to give the group from Mobile any support they needed. The public was waiting for the submarine to sink one of the Union ironclads that immobilized the harbor. John Fraser & Co. offered $100,000 for the destruction of the *Ironside* and a similar sum for the sinking of the wooden frigate *Wabash*.

Eager to be in action, the submariners set up in a cove behind Fort Moultrie and set to work. Horace Hunley was off on another mission but he wrote McClintock about his hopes.

"It is not at all a question of whether you will succeed in blowing up a vessel of the enemy, but whether you will make a real, solid contribution to the Confederacy and confer glory on its originators."

Hunley arrived in Charleston on August 20 to discover that his submariners had spent their first week going out on several missions without success. The military men began to complain:

"The torpedo boat started at sunset but returned because (they said) of an accident. Whitney says that although McClintock is timid they shall go tonight unless the weather is bad."

But it seemed the weather was always bad, or they suffered some failure of equipment, or someone got sick, so the days went by and there were no attacks.

General Clingman, the commander of Sullivan's Island, lost confidence.

"The torpedo boat has not gone out. I do not think it will render any service under its present management."

General Beauregard, too, lost confidence in the crew. The navy offered an officer to be attached to the boat, but Hunley refused because, he claimed, an inexperienced hand would hinder rather than help their efforts.

Finally Beauregard ordered the boat seized and the civilian crew replaced by volunteers from the Confederate navy. Lt. John Payne was put in command. He was as reckless as McClintock was cautious, but

Sketch of the Hunley, *made by Conrad Wise Chapman on December 2, 1863, in preparation for his painting.* Courtesy Valentine Richmond History Center.

authority regarded this as a plus factor. He brought to the boat his good friend Lt. Charles Hasker and four other men: Michael Cane, Nicholas Davis, Frank Doyle, and John Kelly joined Absolum Williams, Charles Sprague, and Jeremiah Donovan.

The one who worried most about the change was the dispossessed Captain McClintock.

"The boat and machinery was so very simple," he said, "that many persons at first inspection believed they could work the boat without practice, or experience, and although I endeavored to prevent inexperienced persons from going under water in the craft, I was not always successful in preventing them."

Captain Tucker and General Beauregard were among those who believed the operation of the submarine was a simple matter, and they urged action on Lt. Payne and his crew. Payne rushed the crew through several swift-training sessions. On August 29, 1863, just a day or two after taking command, Payne held several training sessions and dives, anticipating making an attack that evening. That afternoon the submarine was moored at the dock near Fort Johnson on the south end of the bay.

That evening as they prepared to depart Payne was climbing into the forward hatchway, preparing to shove off. He gave the order to go ahead, and the crew cranked the boat forward. Then as he was climbing through the hatch he became caught in the mooring line. Trying to clear himself, the lieutenant got his foot caught on the lever that controlled the fins, and depressed the lever for a dive. The hatches were still open; the boat dived and began to fill rapidly. Lt. Payne escaped through the forward hatchway, and Donovan and Sprague scrambled out of the after hatch as the submarine went down. Lt. Hasker described what happened next:

> Six of us went down with the boat. I had to get over the bar that connected the fins and through the column of water which was rapidly filling the boat. The manhole plate came down on my back; but I worked my way out until my left leg was caught by the plate, pressing the calf of my leg in two. Held in this manner, I was carried to the bottom in forty-two feet of water. When the boat touched bottom I felt the pressure relax. Stooping down, I took hold of the manhole plate, drew out my wounded limb, and swam to the surface.

The other five members of the crew went down with the boat to a watery grave.

The submarine was recovered by two civilian divers, Angus Smith and David Broadfoot. It was a difficult and perilous undertaking: The submarine was stuck fast in the mud, and the divers had to tunnel their way through below the keel in order to wrap the boat in heavy chains. Finally the boat came up to reveal its ghastly cargo of bloated, decomposed bodies. Rigor mortis had set in, and to retrieve the bodies for burial the rescuers had to saw them apart.

Hunley came to oversee the submarine's salvage and refit. On September 19 he wrote General Beauregard requesting that the salvaged vessel be placed under his control, and that he be allowed to bring an experienced crew from Mobile to man it.

Beauregard thought that an excellent idea, and so Hunley regained control of his own boat. But he did not get command: The general did not have that much confidence in his seamanship. Command went to Lt George Dixon, a six-foot blond Adonis who had commanded the boat during trials at Mobile. Dixon had enlisted early in the war in Company A of the 21st Alabama Infantry. When the regiment marched off to war, his sweetheart, Queenie Bennett, came to the train station to say goodbye. She pressed a twenty-dollar gold piece into his hand.

Dixon later fought in the Battle of Shiloh and was one of the 23,000 casualties of this battle. Struck in the left thigh by a Yankee bullet, Dixon had Queenie's gold piece in his pocket—and the bullet did not penetrate his leg. He had the coin inscribed on the reverse:

Shiloh.
April 6th 1862.
My life preserver.
G.E.D.

For the rest of his life Dixon would carry his good-luck piece.

Most of the rest of the new crew came from Mobile:

Thomas Park
Henry Beard
Robert Brookbank
John Marshall
Charles McHugh
Joseph Patterson

They were joined by Charles Sprague, who had survived the sinking of August 29.

By the first week of October the new crew had assembled in the refurbished submarine on the Cooper River. Lt Dixon was in command, operating the forward diving planes, and Park was second in command, handling the ballast tanks and sea valves. A new compass had been installed, along with 200 feet of rope to tow a torpedo.

The sub made many practice dives under the tender *Indian Chief* and in two weeks seemed to be ready for action.

The morning of October 15, 1863, dawned gray and drizzly. The sub left the dock at 9:25 and within two minutes was near the *Indian Chief.* Hunley was in command of his own ship because Lt Dixon was out of town.

Nearing the tender, Hunley took one final reading, the hatches were battened down, the diving planes depressed, and the submarine slowly went down.

Then there was silence. Aboard the *Indian Chief,* after a few minutes they knew that something had gone wrong. The submarine did not come up

They waited. A few bubbles came up, but that was all.

By noon the sad truth had to be told. The submarine was lost.

Once more divers Smith and Broadfoot were called.

On October 18 they found the wreck in 54 feet of water, bow-down, stuck in the harbor mud. Rescue operations were delayed when a storm blew up and it was three and a half weeks before the submarine was raised. Inside, the scene truly represented the terror that had overcome the crew; some clutched candles, apparently trying to force open the hatches, some lay on the bottom, all together. Captain Hunley's body was forward with his head in the forward hatchway, his right hand on top of his head, as if he had been trying to raise the hatch cover. In his left hand was a new candle. The seacock near him was wide open, and the cock wrench was lying on the bottom of the boat.

First Officer Park was found lying in the after hatchway, his right hand above his head. He had been trying to raise the hatch cover. The seacock to his ballast tank was closed. The other bodies were floating in the water. The bolts that held the iron keel in place had been half turned, but not enough to release the ballast. Hunley had obviously dropped the valve handle by accident and in the darkness could not see to retrieve it. He had then exhausted himself at the pump, water flowing in through the open valve faster than he could pump it out.

On Sunday, November 8, 1863, the Rev W. B. Yates performed the Episcopal funeral. General Beauregard had ordered full military honors, so the cortege included two companies of troops and a band. The procession wound its way through the Charleston streets to Magnolia Cemetery, followed by a large number of citizens. Next day the crew members were buried in an adjacent plot.

The surviving crewmen named the boat in honor of their fallen comrade. It was now the *H. L. Hunley.* Most people were reverential when they discussed the *Hunley* and its troubles, but the sailors and soldiers of Charleston had a new name for the submarine: "the murdering machine."

Hunley's death changed General Beauregard's enthusiasm to despair, and he vowed to have no more to do with a device that "is more dangerous to those who use it than to the enemy." Lt. Dixon was ordered back to Mobile and was supposed to rejoin his military unit, but he pleaded the case of the submarine's usefulness, and finally General Beauregard relented. The *Hunley* would be given one more chance to prove its worth. By the second week of November Dixon was back in Charleston, with two associates, Henry Dillingham and Lt. William Alexander.

The Hunley *sinks for a second time, with its bow stuck in the mud of Charleston Harbor, killing Horace Hunley and his crew.* Illustration by Daniel Dowdey, South Carolina State Museum.

First he ordered cleaning supplies, to remove the smell of death, and a crew of seamen set to work to put the boat to rights.

The *Hunley* was put up on cradles on a dock in Mt Pleasant, a harbor town northwest of Sullivan's Island, for a refit that was finished at the end of November. Now came the hard part: General Beauregard had no confidence in the submarine, and hesitated to risk any more lives. But after much persuasion from Lt. Dixon the general agreed to let him go aboard the receiving ship *Indian Chief* and call for volunteers. There was no difficulty. Dixon had all the volunteers he needed. He selected five men: Arnold Becker, F. Collins, Joseph Ridgeway, C. Simkins, and James A. Wicks. They would join the group from Mobile: Dixon, Alexander, Dillingham, and one unknown—brave men, all. Wicks, for example, had a wife and four daughters.

"But I don't believe a man considered the danger," Lt. Alexander wrote later. "The honor of being first to engage the enemy in this novel way overshadowed all else."

They took up quarters at the Old Shell Hall on Ferry Street in Mt. Pleasant and began training, although the submarine was still up in its cradle.

Soon the boat was ready for practice dives, and by early December Dixon felt confident enough to announce that the *Hunley* was ready for action. On December 14 General Beauregard issued a special order to Dixon to proceed to the mouth of the harbor and sink any vessel with which he came into contact.

Admiral Dahlgren, commander of the blockading fleet, had recently issued a new directive ordering the ironclads to observe new safety precautions against torpedo boats, which included moving them in the harbor and setting up torpedo nets. This changed the game for Dixon. He turned to the squadron of wooden warships anchored farther out, and relocated the *Hunley*'s base to Battery Marshall on the eastern end of Sullivan's Island. He also changed the armament of the *Hunley*. She would not tow a torpedo but would attack with a spar torpedo fitted onto her prow.

In the early part of January 1864, the men of the Hunley practiced every afternoon at about one o'clock, walking on the beach seven miles to Battery Marshall and taking the *Hunley* out for two or three hours of diving practice. Dixon and Alexander would stretch out on the beach with the compass between them and plot a course to the nearest ship, the torpedo would be shipped up, and when darkness came they would go out, steering for their target, and continuing until forced by circumstance to start home. They made no attacks, because something always seemed to go wrong with tides, moonlight, or the condition of the men. But they did gain stamina through these exercises, and once when they had trouble with the pumps they managed to stay under water for two hours and thirty-five minutes. So long were they under water that their navy comrades had given them up for lost; General Beauregard was informed that the submarine had been sunk. It was only the following day, when the entire crew showed up at headquarters, that he would believe they were still alive. After accepting the general's congratulations on not being dead, Lt. Dixon reassured him that they would attack an enemy vessel as soon as possible. And they went back to practicing. In smooth water and light wind and current the *Hunley* could make about four miles an hour, but this was winter and the weather was usually foul so they had to go out with the ebb tide and come in with the flood. They needed a dark night, too, because they had to surface often to check position.

Early in February Lt. Alexander and Dillingham were recalled to Mobile for special duty, to help build a breech-loading repeating cannon. It was a terrible shock losing two of their small crew, but volunteers showed up from the South Carolina Light Artillery, one named C. F. Carlson and the other Miller, both German immigrants. Within a couple of weeks the *Hunley* crew was almost back to normal.

Then, in the third week of February, they finally got their target.

4

ATTACK ON THE *HOUSATONIC*

THE NEW TARGET of the *Hunley* was the United States screw sloop of war *Housatonic,* which was moored three miles off Rattlesnake Shoal, near Battery Marshall. She was 207 feet long, 38 feet in the beam, and displaced 1,240 tons. Built at the Boston Navy Yard and launched on November 29, 1861, she carried a formidable arsenal: one 100-pound and three thirty pound Parrott rifles, an eleven-inch Dahlgren smoothbore, two 32-pound smooth-bores, and three howitzers. She was commanded by Captain John Pickering and had joined the South Atlantic Blockading Squadron in September 1862; she was a famil-iar sight in Charleston. She had already proved her worth to the Union cause, engaging the Confederate rams *Chicora* and *Palmetto State* in their attack on January 31, 1863, and occasionally landing raiding parties to attack Charleston's outer defenses. Recently she had captured several blockade runners. Every night she anchored at

Rattlesnake Shoal, gun crews and boilers ready for any Confederate vessel that should try to slip past.

All that was needed was a calm, clear night, and on February 17, they got it. The sea was flat, no wind, and the moon was shining as they boarded the submarine and

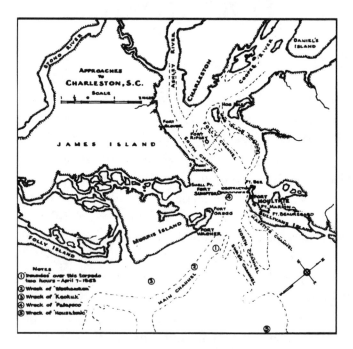

Chart of approaches to Charleston, showing wrecks of various U.S. Navy ships, including the Housatonic *(number 5, lower right corner). The* Hunley *was discovered some 350 meters to the east of the* Housatonic. Redrawn from "Official Records of the Union and Confederate Navies." Courtesy Naval Historical Center.

wriggled through the narrow hatches. Lt. Dixon had arranged with the commander of Battery Marshall that if they succeeded in their dangerous mission, they would show two blue lights as they returned; the battery would respond with a beacon to guide the submarine back to Breach Inlet. The crewmen worked their way past melted candle wax left over from previous voyages, and drops of condensation on the bulkheads, to their places: Dixon at the command post, one of the other eight at Lt. Alexander's position at the rear hatch, and the rest at the cranks.

USS Housatonic, *in a drawing by R. G. Skerrett in 1902.* Courtesy Naval Historical Center.

The men cranked steadily for an hour, Dixon stopping occasionally to keep them on course. When the submarine was within striking distance of the *Housatonic,* he brought her up for one last observation, and then quickly submerged again. It was now about 8:45 P.M. Aboard the *Housatonic,* the crew was in an alert condition, with lookouts on the forecastle, gangways, and quarterdeck. From his station on the quarterdeck Acting Master John K. Crosby saw an object approaching—at first it seemed like a porpoise. The quartermaster looked through his glass and said it looked like a school of fish.

Suddenly Crosby recognized the outline—it appeared to be a Confederate torpedo boat.

He sounded the alarm and ordered the anchor chain slipped. Officers and men came on deck in a hurry, firing pistols and rifles.

Captain Pickering was in the cabin examining a book of charts. Assistant Surgeon Platt was sitting a the table with him. Suddenly the captain heard a confused sound that indicated some excitement on deck. He jumped up, thinking a blockade runner must have been sighted. In his haste he picked up Surgeon Platt's cap, got halfway to the cabin door when he saw his error and went back to exchange the cap for his own, returned to the door, passing the orderly who was waiting there without speaking, and made his way on deck. He gave the order to slip the anchor and go astern, and to open fire with the guns. But the guns could not be depressed to cover the *Hunley*, which was now nearly upon the ship. The captain picked up a double-barreled shotgun loaded with buckshot and jumped up on the horse block on the starboard quarter, which had just been vacated by the first lieutenant after firing a musket at the submarine.

The captain looked down and saw the *Hunley*, a gray shape just a few feet off the starboard quarter abreast of the mizzenmast. He made out two projections above the water—the hatch covers—fired his shotgun at them, jumped down from the horse block, and ran up the port side of the quarterdeck as far as the mizzenmast.

"Go astern faster," he ordered. He noticed that the men were huddled forward, but he did not call them to the guns because he knew the guns would not depress until the ship had made some sternway, putting distance between it and the submarine.

> I thought of going forward myself to get clear of the torpedo, but reflecting that my proper station was aft, I remained where I was and the next instant was blown from there and found myself in the water about where I had stood before the explosion, among broken timbers, the debris of panel work and planking. I succeeded in getting into the mizzen rigging very much bruised. And was eventually rescued by a boat. The ship was then lying on its port side. I do

not know the interval of time between the explosion and my getting into the rigging.

Neither did the captain know that it had taken less than five minutes for his ship to sink to the bottom.

The ship *Canandaigua,* which was anchored nearby, hoisted distress signals and came to help. The *Housatonic* settled down on the shallow bottom, its masts standing up in the sky.

The submarine crashed into the *Housatonic* with a tremendous impact, the barbed head of the spar torpedo entering the hull below the waterline on the starboard side, just forward of the mizzenmast. The *Hunley* reversed course and the line played out from the harpoon warhead, until Lt. Dixon pulled the lanyard and the air was rent with a tremendous explosion. A hole appeared in the starboard side of the *Housatonic,* and splinters of wood shot into the sky. Landsman Theodore Parker was standing lookout directly above the point of impact and was killed instantly, his body flung high in the air.

One crewman described the blast: "Rather sharp. I saw a very large quantity of black smoke, but no column of water and no flame."

"The explosion knocked me off my feet, as if the ship had struck hard on the bottom," said another crewman. "I saw fragments of the wreck going up in the air, but no

The Hunley's *spar torpedo detonates against the starboard stern quarter of the* Housatonic. Illustration by Daniel Dowdey, South Carolina State Museum.

column of water, no smoke, and no flame. It was as if we had collided with another vessel."

"I heard a report like the distant firing of a howitzer," said Ensign C. H. Craven. "The ship went down by the stern, and three or four minutes after the stern was submerged, the whole ship was submerged."

As the *Housatonic* went down the scenes were dramatic beyond compare—men with nothing on but their shirts struggling in the water, officers trying to get the boats free, others climbing into the rigging.

Quartermaster John Williams, captain's clerk Charles O. Mazzey, and John Walsh drowned. Walsh, a foretopman from Boston, had gotten safely to the deck but went back below to get $30 he had hidden in a bag on the berth deck. Ensign E. L. Hazeltine left the safety of a launch to jump back aboard the ship as it keeled over. The last seen of him was his corpse floating in the water.

Survivors clambered into the rigging and remained until plucked off. A stream of disheveled officers and crewmen, many of them naked, were hauled aboard the *Canandaigua* and given blankets, hot coffee, and medical attention. Many were transferred from the *Canandaigua* to the *Wabash*.

The death toll was five dead, two injured, and one warship sunk. Captain Pickering was so badly hurt by the blast and his exposure in the rigging that he could not function and had to turn management of the crew over to Executive Officer Higginson.

5

THE FATE
OF THE *HUNLEY*

AND WHAT HAPPENED to the *Hunley?*

After Lt. Dixon reversed course, she backed away from the *Housatonic* and the explosion of the spar torpedo. When Lt. Dixon believed she was safe, he hoisted a blue lantern at the forward hatch and ordered his second in command to hoist one at the after hatch. Thus he kept his promise to Battery Marshall to inform them of his success. The sinking had been observed from shore and the battery, in turn, lighted a beacon to show the *Hunley* the way home.

But hours passed and the *Hunley* did not appear at Sullivan's Island. The hours became days, and still the *Hunley* did not appear, nor did the defenders of Charleston know the name of the vessel she had sunk. Then a Union picket boat passed too close to Fort Sumter and was captured. Interrogation of the crew revealed that the vessel sunk was the *Housatonic,* and that five crewmen had been killed. The next day General Beauregard sent a telegram to Richmond.

> Prisoners report that it was the ship of war *Housatonic* 12 guns, which was sunk on the night of 17th instantly by the submarine torpedo boat. Lt. Dixon, of Alabama, commanding. There is little hope of the safety of that brave man and his associates, however, as they were not captured.

In Mobile, Lt. Alexander read in the newspapers an account of the *Hunley*'s accomplishment and was deeply disappointed that he had been assigned to other duty and had missed the chance for glory. Still, when he noted that there was no mention of the fate of the submarine, his disappointment was somewhat tempered. He wired General Jordan in Charleston every day asking for information. Each reply was the same.

"No news."

"After much thought," Alexander concluded, "I decided that Dixon had been unable to work his way back against the wind and the tide and the *Hunley* must have been carried out to sea."

Henry Leovy, the executor of the estate of Horace Hunley, heard rumors of the destruction of the *Housatonic*. On March 5 he wrote to General Beauregard requesting confirmation of the story and the status of the submarine of which he said he was part owner.

"I am exceedingly anxious to learn whether Lt. Dixon accomplished his gallant act with our boat or not, and whether he has escaped. It will be a source of pride to me to learn this."

Five days later an officer on Beauregard's staff responded to Leovy's request for more information:

Sir:

I am directed by the commanding general to inform you that it is the torpedo boat H L *Hunley* that destroyed the Federal man of war *Housatonic* and that Lt. Dixon commanded the expedition but I regret to say that nothing has been heard either of Lt Dixon or the torpedo boat. It is therefore feared that gallant officer and his brave companions have perished.

The commanding officer of the Mobile defenses, General Maury, was also interested in the fate of the submarine and inquired of General Beauregard's headquarters. Several weeks passed with no real answer. On April 29, Captain Grey of the Charleston Torpedo Service informed the general as to what he believed was the fate of the *Hunley.*

In answer to a communication of yours, received through headquarters, relative to Lt. Dixon and crew I was not informed as to the service in which

Lt. Dixon was engaged or under what orders he was acting. I am informed that he requested Commodore Tucker to furnish him some men, which he did. Their names are as follows, Viz: Arnold Becker, C Simkins, James A Wicks, F Collins, and Noname Ridgeway of the Navy and Cpl. C. F. Carlson of Captain Wagner's company of artillery.

The United States sloop of war was attacked and destroyed on the night of February 17. Since that time no information had been received, of either the boat or its crew. I am of the opinion that the torpedo being placed at the bow of the boat, she went into the hole made in the *Housatonic* by the explosion and did not have sufficient power to back out, consequently sunk with her.

Thus was born the conventional wisdom that surrounded the fate of the *Hunley* for many years.

AFTERMATH

It was three days after the sinking of the *Housatonic* that the wreck was spotted from the ramparts of Battery Marshall, because so many tugs and barges were milling about the sunken vessel. Within an hour of the sighting, Colonel Dantzler, commander of the battery, sent word to Beauregard's headquarters. While Beauregard and his staff pondered the whereabouts of the

missing *Hunley,* federal sea captains along the South
Carolina coast had warnings from Admiral Dahlgren's
headquarters:

> The *Housatonic* had been torpedoed by a Rebel
> *David* and sunk almost instantly. It was at night and
> the water smooth. The success of this undertaking
> will, no doubt, lead to similar attempts along the line
> of the blockade. If ships are resting at anchor they are
> presumed unsafe, particularly in smooth water, with-
> out outriggers and hawsers stretched around, with
> rope netting dropped into the water. Vessels on inside
> blockade had better take post outside at night and
> keep under way, until these precautions are completed.

Furthermore, the admiral warned, "Ship's boats must
be on patrol when the vessel is not in movement. Com-
manders are required to use the utmost vigilance—nothing else will serve."

Nine days after the sinking Confederate authorities still
did not know the identity of the ship sunk. As noted previously, it was finally learned when a Union picket boat
was captured by the *Indian Chief.*

One of the sailors aboard the *Indian Chief* wrote to a
friend in Alabama:

> A few nights ago a party of a dozen men went out in
> a submarine boat, in which they could remain

underwater for an hour or so, and struck a large vessel with a torpedo, and blew the bottom out of her.

The news of the sinking of the *Housatonic* spread through Charleston like wildfire. It was just what the exhausted population needed—a victory to celebrate. The February 29 edition of the *Charleston Mercury* had an account:

As a practical and important result of this splendid achievement, the prisoners state that all the wooden vessels of the blockading squadron now go far out to sea every night, being afraid of riding in any portion of the outer harbor.

6

COURT OF INQUIRY

WHENEVER A U.S. NAVAL vessel is damaged or lost the law requires a court of inquiry, to fix responsibility and discover if negligence of duty was involved. The court of inquiry into the sinking of the *Housatonic* was convened on February 26, 1864, aboard the squadron flagship *Wabash*. The members of the court were: Captain J. F. Green, Captain Jonathan DeCamp, and Commander J. L. Williamson. Judge advocate was Lt. James B. Young of the marine corps.

Master John Crosby was the first witness called. He testified that he had taken the deck at 8 P.M. on February 17.

> At about 8:45 I saw something on the water which looked at first like a porpoise coming up to the surface to blow. It was about 45 yards from us on our starboard beam. I called the quartermaster's attention to it, asking him if he saw it but he said he saw nothing but a ripple in the water.

Looking again I saw that it was coming toward the ship very fast. I gave orders to beat to quarters, slip the chain and back the engine. At this time, the Officer of the Forecastle, Acting Masters Mate Corinthwaite, came aft and reported seeing this object on the water. I informed the captain that I had seen something on the water coming towards the ship very fast, but could not make out what it was.

About this time the executive officer, Lt. Higginson, came on the bridge and asked me what it was. I told him I could not tell.

Captain Pickering came on deck, ordered the anchor slipped and the engine reversed and asked me what I had seen.

Crosby repeated that he had seen something but could not identify it. Then he left the bridge, the executive officer having taken over, and went forward to see if the chain had been slipped. As he was coming aft again the explosion occurred.

After he gave the order to go to quarters several muskets were fired at the object, and when it was close alongside, Captain Pickering fired his shotgun at it.

I don't think it was over two and a half minutes from the time I first saw the object when it struck and the explosion took place.

I was abreast of the engine room hatch on the starboard side, I jumped over to the port side and into the dinghy and gave orders to the men around me to help clear it away. I cut the falls but while clearing it away the ship rolled heavily to port and the dinghy swamped. The ship commenced filling as soon as the explosion took place and was full of water and on the bottom when she lurched heavily to port, all this occupying about a minute and a half. After the dingy swamped I jumped into the rigging, went up to the mizzen top and down the starboard side. I took four men, cleared away the third cutter and started to pick up men in the water. After I had picked up the men I pulled towards the ship again, took two men off some pieces of deck that lay close to the ship's quarter. At this time I heard Captain Pickering's voice in the port mizzen rigging. He told me to take him out of the rigging and pull for the *Canandaigua,* he afterwards said "Pick up all the officers and men you can find in the water who are in danger before you come to me."

I obeyed the orders and took him out of the rigging and started for the *Canandaigua.* When I picked these men up in the water all the rest of the officers and men had got into the fore and mizzen rigging. They were unable to clear away the launches as they were in iron cranes and could not be got out in time. The 4th cutter and dingy were swamped when she lurched to port. Before I got to the *Canandaigua* she had slipped and was standing toward the wreck. I went alongside, put men aboard, got a fresh crew, and started back for the wreck, with boats from the *Canandaiga* and took two boatloads of men to her.

The court asked questions about the number of lookouts on duty as well as the number and placement of officers on the deck on duty at the time.

Crosby testified that there were three lookouts on each side of the ship: the quartermaster on the quarter deck, the officer of the forecastle on the forecastle, and the officer of the deck on the bridge.

As to the attacker, it looked to Crosby to be about 30 feet long and four feet wide, like a whale boat capsized.

Why did he order the engine backed? "To avoid fouling the propeller with the slip rope." As to sternboard, he thought there was very little when the missile struck.

No gun could be brought to bear on the submarine because they would not depress and there was no time to train one.

Was the ship ready for action?

Yes, in Master Crosby's opinion, it was.

As for Captain Pickering, that brave soul had hung in the mizzen rigging to the point of exhaustion, refusing to be picked up before all those in peril had been rescued.

There was no panic, perfect discipline had been maintained, everything possible had been done to prevent the attack and preserve the ship.

The inquiry was adjourned to the *Canandaigua,* to hear the testimony of Captain Pickering. He told his story of the attack and sinking of his ship. His was the last testimony to be heard, and on Monday, March 7, the court met again on the *Wabash.*

The decision:

1. The US Steamer *Housatonic* was blown up and sunk by a rebel torpedo craft on the night of February 17, 1864, at about 9 P.M. while lying at anchor in 24 feet of water off Charleston, S.C. The weather at the time was clear the night being bright and moonlit, wind moderate from the north and west, sea smooth and tide half ebb, the ship heading WNW, that between 8:45 and 9 P.M. an object was discovered in the water almost simultaneously by the officer of the deck and the lookout on the starboard cathead, at about 75 yards distant, having the appearance of a log.

2. That on further and closer observation, it presented a suspicious appearance, moved apparently with a speed of 3.5–4 knots in the direction of the starboard quarter of the ship, exhibiting two protuberances above and making a slight ripple in the water.

3. That the strange object approached the ship with rapidity, precluding a gun of the battery being brought to bear upon it and finally came into contact with the ship on her starboard quarter.

4. That about one and a half minutes after the first discovery, the crew were called to quarters, the cable slipped, and the engine backed.

5. That an explosion occurred about three minutes after the first discovery of the object which blew up the after part of the ship; causing her to sink immediately after to the bottom with her spar deck submerged.

6. That several shots from small arms were fired at the object while it was alongside the ship before the explosion occurred.

7. That the watch on deck, ship and ships battery were in all respects prepared for sudden offensive or defensive movement, that lookouts were properly stationed, and vigilance observed, and that officers and men promptly assembled at the call to quarters.

8. That order was preserved on board and orders promptly obeyed by officers and men up to the time of the sinking of the ship.

In view of the above facts the Court has to express the opinion that no further military proceedings are necessary.

THE FATE OF THE SEA

THE CONVENTIONAL WISDOM in Charleston was that the *Hunley* had been the victim of her own success. She would be found, said the pundits, mixed in the wreckage of the *Housatonic*.

But a few facts were known to the men of Battery Marshall to whom the *Hunley* had shown two blue lights. Battery Marshall had responded with a beacon, which they kept going all night long in the hope, finally forlorn, that the *Hunley* would turn up.

Speculation continued, but now it was certain, said General Beauregard, that the crew of the submarine had met a watery death.

Still, rumors continued. The *Hunley* had sailed to some foreign port was one. She had been captured, was another. Queenie Bennett waited and hoped for her lover against all hope. There came no hopeful word. Lt. Dixon was lost at sea, and with him the other eight gallant members of the *Hunley* crew.

Nine months after the sinking Lt. W. L. Churchill investigated the *Housatonic* wreck in the schooner *G. W. Blunt*. His report:

The *Housatonic* is very much worm-eaten, as I find from pieces which have been brought up. She is in an upright position, has settled in the sand about five feet, forming a bank of mud and sand around her bed, the mud has collected on her in small quantities. The cabin is completely demolished, as are the bulkheads abaft the mainmast, the coal is scattered about her lower decks in heaps, as well as muskets, small arms and quantities of rubbish.

I tried to find the magazine but the weather has been so unfavorable and the swell, so great that it is not safe to keep a diver on the wreck. I took advantage of all the good weather that I had and examined as much as was possible.

The propeller is in an upright position, the shaft appears to be broken. The rudder post and rudder have been partly blown off, the upper parts of both are in their proper places, while the lower parts have been forced aft.

The stern frame rests upon the rudder post and propeller and part of it can be easily slung with chain slings , and a powerful steamer can detach each part.

And did Lt. Churchill find the *Hunley*?

I have caused the bottom to be dragged to an area of 500 yards around the wreck, finding nothing of the torpedo boat. On the 24th the drag ropes caught something heavy. On sending a diver down to examine it, it proved to be a quantity of rubbish. This examination being completed I could accomplish nothing further, unless it is the intention to raise the wreck or propeller, in which case it will be necessary to have more machinery.

Nothing of the submarine, no trace.

But at least it was now established where the submarine was not.

On October 8, 1870, the *Charleston Daily Republican* remembered the *Hunley*.

We all know the fate of the brave *Housatonic*. Brave Dixon guided his torpedo fairly against her, the explosion tore up the great ship's sides, so that she went down with all her crew in two minutes. [That this statement was not true did not bother the *Republican*'s editorialist.]

The torpedo vessel also disappeared forever from mortal view. Whether she went down with her enemy or whether she drifted out to sea to bury her dead was never known, and their fate was left to the great day when the sea shall give up her dead.

But within a few weeks past, divers in submarine armor have visited the wreck of the *Housatonic,* and they have found the little vessel lying by her huge victim and within are the bones of the most daring and devoted men who ever went to war.

Angus Smith, the salvage diver who had twice brought the *Hunley* up to the surface, was the source of this remarkable story. (Smith was under contract to the city of Charleston to raise wrecks in Charleston Harbor. What he expected to do when his fabrication was exposed was never revealed.)

Subsequent years were full of hoaxes, fabrications, and rumors. Showman Phineas T. Barnum offered the then staggering sum of $100,000 to anyone who would produce the *Hunley* for display in his famous New York City museum. Nobody appeared to claim the offer. Meanwhile the principal characters of this sea drama were dying off. Queenie Bennett languished for a while, but recovered to marry a childhood friend.

For more than a hundred years the *Hunley* lay unmolested on the ocean floor, even its location unknown. Occasionally a curious treasure hunter would take a look for the submarine, but nothing ever came of such casual expeditions. And until the middle of the 20th Century, no one cared enough to pursue the matter.

With the end of the Civil War the world forgot the *Housatonic* and the *Hunley.*

The broken hulk of the former would remain a menace to navigation for another nine years, until its rotten superstructure was demolished in the summer of 1873 and the remains moved to deeper water off Sullivan's Island. After that, for 36 years a marker buoy gave the location. In February 1909 the remains of the wreck were dynamited and destroyed. Boats were finally freed to navigate around the site. Over the next few years the remains of the *Housatonic* were covered by sand and ignored by the world.

THE SEARCH
FOR THE *HUNLEY*

THE SEARCH FOR the *Hunley* began in earnest in the 1970s. The principals in the drama were Edward Lee Spence, Mark Newell, and wealthy writer Clive Cussler, author of many popular adventure stories.

Spence had known the story of the *Hunley* since boyhood. He became seriously interested in the *Hunley* in the fall of 1970 when he and friends were fishing in Charleston Harbor and one of the fish traps got hung up on an underwater obstruction. Spence had his diving gear along, so he stripped down to his underwear and went overboard to free the trap.

When he reached the bottom he saw a long cylindrical object half buried in the silt. The trap got loose and was hauled to the surface. Spence became nervous at being under water in strange surroundings alone and so he also went up, shouting, "The *Hunley*, I've found her!"

Newell became interested in the *Hunley* in the 1960s when he studied the records of the sinking of the *Housatonic* and learned that the *Hunley* had shown two blue lights to Battery Marshall *after* the sinking. He postulated that Lt. Dixon had headed the submarine for Maffitt's Channel on its way home and had sunk somewhere in between the wreck of the *Housatonic* and the channel. His interest became serious in 1994 when he was writing a Ph.D. thesis for his doctorate at Scotland's St. Andrews University. But in 1880, to improve Charleston Harbor, large granite jetties had been built in Maffitt's Channel, necessitating the use of ship-towed metal detectors to find anything under the silt that had piled up. Such an enterprise was far beyond Newell's means.

Cussler had become interested in the *Hunley* in 1980, seeking material for his books. In that year and the following, he organized searches for the submarine, with no success.

Newell approached Cussler, who agreed to organize a search by his National Underwater and Marine Agency (NUMA). The search covered about 50 square miles of ocean off Charleston Harbor. In the last days of the search they found an object matching the known size and mass of the *Hunley* in the spot Newell had predicted, the approach to Maffitt's Channel, just outside Charleston Harbor. It was a logical place for the *Hunley* to be but, it was later learned during an *ad hoc* NUMA dive, it wasn't the *Hunley*.

On May 3, 1995, divers Wes Hall, Ralph Wilbanks, and Harry Pecorelli, in the employ of Cussler's NUMA, decided to reexamine one of the sites that previously had been identified as showing something metallic under the sand. The site was not wholly promising, being several hundred yards farther out to sea than the site of the old *Housatonic* wreck. But they decided to cover all bases and took a look. Pecorelli began the probe, followed by Hall. By luck they had begun pushing away sand just over the forward hatch of the *Hunley*. It was an identifying characteristic too unique to the *Hunley* to be anything else. They knew they had found it at last.

The news broke on May 11. Cussler announced that eight days earlier his search team had found the *Hunley* four miles off Sullivan's Island, resting under thirty feet of water.

Glenn McConnell was a Civil War reenacter and owner of a Civil War history and art shop in Charleston. He was also a South Carolina state senator. He was on the floor of the South Carolina Senate in Columbia "when the news came that the *Hunley* had been found. It was like a bell going off," he said.

The U.S. Navy immediately claimed ownership of the *Hunley,* under the principle of sovereign immunity as extended to the properties of the Confederate States of America. Dr. Robert Neyland of the Navy Historical

Center explored this concept in a paper published in 2001, which was written to clarify the navy position relative to the *Hunley.*

Under this policy the Department of the Navy retains ownership of ship and aircraft wrecks despite the passage of time and regardless of where the entity was lost. These wrecks are not abandoned but remain the property of the government until a specific formal action is taken to dispose of them. They are thus immune from the law of salvage; no salvage is permitted without express authorization from the navy. This immunity is founded on long-existing historic principles of maritime law.

Navy custody of these wrecks is based on the property clause of the U.S. Constitution, Articles 95 and 96 of the United Nations Convention Law of the Sea, and established principles of international maritime law. These laws establish that the right, title, or ownership of federal property is not lost to the government due to the passage of time, or by neglect or inaction. Ultimately abandonment of government-owned ships and aircraft occurs only through congressional action. A coastal state does not acquire ownership of sunken warships even though the wrecks are located in state waters.

In the court decision *United States v. Steinmetz,* concerning ownership of the bell of the CSS *Alabama,* the wreck of that famous raider was not considered abandoned by the mere passage of time. The court held that the United

States rightfully succeeded to the ownership of the property of the Confederacy. The Union had actually, despite all the propaganda, dealt with the Confederacy as a sovereign nation.

Where human remains are concerned, as had generally been assumed was the case with the *Hunley,* U.S. naval policy is clear: "As a matter of policy the government does not grant permission to salvage ships that contain the bodies of the servicemen. Congress has stipulated that any salvage must provide for the proper burial of the remains of the crew."

Now the U.S. National Park Service and the U.S. Coast Guard got into the act. The park service sent divers to verify the claim, and with high-tech testing ascertained that the hull of the submarine had a cocoon of mud and silt that had protected it from serious corrosion damage. The Coast Guard kept secret the exact coordinates of the site, placed a mile-square no-travel zone around the site, and placed a wire cage around it to discourage looters. Such is the lure of fortune that $50,000 had already been offered for a hatch cover of the submarine.

After the *Hunley* had been found and identified, it had to be protected. The navy, the General Services Administration, the Council on Historic Preservation, the Hunley Commission of South Carolina, and the South Carolina State preservation officer worked out an agreement protecting the *Hunley* from looters and curiosity seekers.

Scientist Robert Neyland had this to say about the discovery of the *Hunley*:

> The recovery of the *Hunley* represents an enormous magnitude of reasoning and forethought. Many questions come to surface that must be answered before any action is taken as this incredible recovery process unfolds. To leave the *Hunley* in the waters just four miles off Sullivan's Island will place her in even deeper peril. Besides the obvious loss of knowledge due to the sea's powerful corrosive forces, the *Hunley* will certainly be desecrated by souvenir hunters, thieves, and plunderers.
>
> Because of the importance of the Hunley Project the research team felt that it would be beneficial to open themselves to the scrutiny of archaeologists from across the world. During November 1999 the Hunley Conservation Symposium was held at Charleston Museum.
>
> *Hunley* is the most difficult composite iron artifact ever undertaken and it is by far the largest and most complex object ever recovered.

Symposium members pored over the current *Hunley* recovery and conservation plans as well as plans for construction and outfitting that would become the Warren L. Lasch Conservation Center. Unanimously the symposium found the recovery and conservation plan absolute, and noted that the lab facility was to be the most flexible and well equipped in the nation.

"*Hunley* is raising the bar for underwater archaeology and conservation," they said:

> In the many painstaking processes, the *Hunley* Recovery has brought us invaluable milestones. And while the recovery of the *Hunley* mostly is an enterprise of historical significance, the feats of underwater planning and engineering have been enormous. Each day brings to our world meaningful and enlightening discoveries, that go far beyond archaeological importance. Discoveries of future reclamation, rescue and other exploratory applications, are staggering.

The *Hunley* was important because it was the first submarine in history to sink an enemy war vessel, a feat not duplicated until World War I. It was also a submerged war grave, and the bodies of the crewmen deserved to be treated with respect. Because of its significance the *Hunley* was already listed on the National Register of Historic Places, and was under consideration for inclusion as a National Historic Landmark.

The agreement gave the state of South Carolina major responsibility in the investigation and recovery of the vessel, conservation of the submarine and its artifacts, appropriate recovery identification and burial of the human remains, exhibition and education with respect to the vessel and artifacts, and overall financing of the Hunley Project.

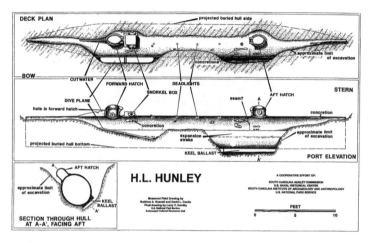

Field drawing of the early stage of the Hunley *excavation, showing the attributes that definitively identified the wreck as the* Hunley. *From field drawing by Matthew A. Russell and David L. Conlin, final drawing by Larry V. Nordby. Courtesy U.S. National Park Service.*

The navy would be accountable for the management of the *Hunley* until transfer to the General Services Administration, which is responsible for the many other Confederate vessels, including the CSS *Alabama*.

Through this agreement the federal government and the state agreed that the *Hunley* would be managed responsibly and displayed in perpetuity in South Carolina.

The Hunley Commission and Hunley Oversight Committee would be responsible to seek advice of professionals in underwater archaeology and conservation.

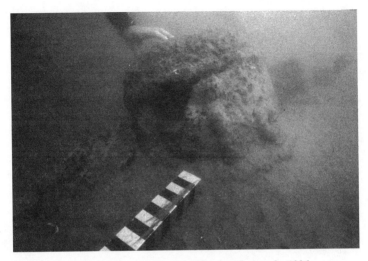

The forward hatch and cutwater of the Hunley *during the 1996 assessment of the site.* (Photo by Christopher F. Amer, South Carolina Institute of Archaeology and Anthropology, University of South Carolina.)

The navy would develop a list of organizations having legitimate interest in the archaeological investigation of the submarine. These organizations would be consulted on proposals for investigation.

The state of South Carolina would receive all legally permissible revenue generated by the curation and display of the *Hunley.*

Almost as soon as this agreement had been drawn, the struggle for credit for the discovery moved into high gear. Edward Spence had spent the intervening years since his original discovery trying to reap some reward from it, without notable success. He had copyrighted everything in sight, and threatened suit against all comers. In 1980 he had filed papers in federal district court to secure owner-ship and salvage rights to the *Housatonic* and the *Hunley*. Asked then to identify where the wreck lay, Spence con-sented only to draw a half-mile circle around the wreck of the *Housatonic,* saying the *Hunley* lay somewhere within it. He claimed that the 1995 discovery by Cussler's divers was nothing but rediscovery of his own feat of fifteen years earlier.

Cussler dismissed his claim and pursued his own course of publicity.

On September 14, 1995, Spence donated all rights to the *Hunley* to the state of South Carolina, although what pre-cisely those rights might be remains a question.

Early in 1997 the Hunley Commission rejected Spence's claim to discovery and accepted Cussler's. In the end, Spence had no witnesses and no hard proof. He *did* have many intriguing points in his favor, but these were not enough for an official commission to nod his way.

Since that time divers from the National Park Service and scientists from the University of South Carolina measured, investigated, and recorded the wreck site. A federal oversight committee was formed to review recov-ery data and three proposals:

- Leave the *Hunley* undisturbed, protecting the site in perpetuity.
- Conduct an underwater archaeological survey and other tests, then rebury the vessel and protect the site.
- Recover the submarine and conduct necessary archaeological and scientific studies and conserve the vessel for future generations.

In the summer of 1999 the last option was chosen. The Hunley Commission accepted a proposal from the Charleston Museum to serve as the *Hunley*'s permanent home and to raise, restore, and care for the boat.

9

RECOVERY

IN THE SUMMER of 1995 the Hunley Project Working Group of the South Carolina Institute of Archaeology and Anthropology (SCIAA) took over management of the *Hunley,* to coordinate the technical expertise and methodology of the salvage. Two national scientific societies and five universities were asked to advise the group in the areas of underwater archaeology, conservation, and ocean engineering.

"The purpose is to ensure that all work on the CSS *H. L. Hunley* is conducted by the most informed team possible," said Dr. Bruce F. Rippeteau, South Carolina state archaeologist and director of the institute. "It is important that the best advisers in our fields of expertise assist us in this historic undertaking. The working group has asked that the Advisory Council for Underwater Archaeology and the American Institute for Conservation of Historic and Artistic Works form blue-ribbon panels to assist them in coordination and implementation of this research."

The Hunley Working Group consisted of three co–principal investigators. Christopher Amer, deputy state archaeologist for underwater archaeology, was given the responsibility of overseeing the underwater archaeology. Dr. Jonathan Leader, deputy state archaeologist and conservator, would coordinate the conservation and stabilization of the vessel. The final co–principal investigator was Dr. William Still, noted author and Civil War historian, who would oversee and coordinate historical research.

The South Carolina Legislature established a state commission to oversee the project, its members to be appointed by the governor and the legislature. The legislature had also taken a strong role in protecting the state's maritime heritage by increasing penalties for unauthorized disturbance of wreck sites that may contain burials and by seeking funds for the continued CSS *H. L. Hunley* research effort.

The University of South Carolina's University Educational Development fund had already then received its first donation for the H. L. Hunley Project from the public. The first check came from the Sons of Confederate Veterans Palmetto Sharpshooters Camp of Anderson, South Carolina.

The governor appointed the commission that summer, with South Carolina state senator Glenn McConnell as chairman.

That summer a downtown walking tour company of Charleston also pledged to donate one dollar to the *Hunley* cause for each person who went on the paid tour.

Charleston's tour company has seen a rise in its business since the TV movie *The Hunley* was shown on Turner television.

"I think it's important to give something back to the history of this beautiful city," said Trae Rhodes, owner of Charleston Walks. "Raising the Confederate submarine *Hunley* and preserving its structural integrity is opportunity to restore a piece of American history that has been missing for over a century. Historians at Charleston are very excited to learn more about the events surrounding its eventual demise so that we can tell the story to those who want to know more."

"Much of the Maritime Tour *revolves* around the story of the waterfront," said John Rosen, the historian responsible for creating this tour. "That's why we are donating to the Friends of the *Hunley* to make sure that the submarine is excavated and cared for properly."

On November 17 the SCIAA reported that several productive meetings had been held with federal and naval authorities, and that author Clive Cussler had released the coordinates of the *Hunley* site.

Dr. William F. Dudley, director of the Naval Historical Center, said this should bring down the cost of expenses for the initial phase of the recovery project.

"The *H. L. Hunley* is a war grave," the SCIAA announced. "Protection and appropriate treatment of the crew's remains has been an important consideration."

On January 4, 1996, the Society for Historical Archaeology held its 29th Conference at Cincinnati. Dr. Dudley and Dr. Robert Neyland held a session on the Civil War. Ralph Wilbanks of NUMA gave a lecture on the search for the *Hunley,* accompanied by 35 minutes of film, and presented evidence of their findings. The video image was viewed through a DOFI Raster screen, which enhanced and enlarged the video images while adding to the depth of field. The lecture and the 1995 NUMA final report combined to present the best evidence to that point of the site being that of the *Hunley.*

Meanwhile the negotiations between the SC Hunley Commission, the federal government, and the navy dragged along. When they were finished it was expected that a program agreement would emerge, but would they ever end?

Disagreements arose over ownership, release of coordinates, the commission's reburial plan, and the proposed site assessment.

The members of the Hunley Commission grew restless and authorized Chairman McConnell to organize an assessment expedition if the negotiations failed. After all, the *Hunley* was at high risk for looting from souvenir hunters.

The Hunley Working Group continued to supply technical support to the Hunley Commission and to provide public information on the progress of the *Hunley* restoration. The commission also persuaded the state government to set up a "Save the Hunley" account to take public contributions.

The threat of the Hunley Commission worked, and when they met February 22, 1996, they could report major headway in settlement of issues with the navy. The commission announced that it hoped to be on the water within 60 days.

The commission invited Ralph Wilbanks, Edward Lee Spence, and Mark Newell to participate in the next proceedings. The State Division of Marine Resources was asked to supply an appropriate boat as stable platform for all the special equipment.

On April 4, 1996, the Hunley Commission approved a $33,000 budget request by the South Carolina Institute of Archaeology and Anthropology for the assessment of the *Hunley* site. This would be conducted by the National Park Service's Submerged Cultural Resource Unit, the Naval Historical Center, and SCIAA with the South Carolina Department of Natural Resources Marine Resources Division. Several private companies were donating equipment. The purpose of the survey would be to confirm the identity of the submarine, document the site, determine the integrity of the hull of the submarine, and make recommendations to the commission regarding future management of the site. The survey began on April 29 and lasted five and a half weeks.

Daniel Lenihan of the National Park Service and Christopher Amer of SCIAA were the principal investigators; Larry Murphy was field director. Security was provided by the Coast Guard, the Naval Weapons Station, and the Naval Criminal Investigative Service.

Several private companies donated their expertise and equipment: Marine Sonic Technology, Edgetech Corporation, Oceaneering Inc., Geometrics Inc., and Sandia Research Associates.

Ralph Wilbanks made the first dive on May 3 and through it discovered that the coordinates named by the NUMA expedition were about forty-two meters off the actuality as established by the Global Positioning System. This difference, which turned out to be a technical glitch growing out of differing GPS systems used, was reconciled and the diving began in earnest.

The initial task was to use water dredges to establish contact with the object. The next step would be to excavate systematically along the hull, to confirm that this was indeed the *Hunley.*

After the two ends of the object were established, a yellow ¼ inch polypropylene line was established down the centerline of the object, for orientation during diving. The line was secured by driving two plastic pipes into the seabed, a meter beyond any buried metal.

A dive team came from the SCIAA, with the 25 foot dive boat *C-Hawk,* to prepare for the arrival of the *Anita,* the primary dive vessel. The daily routine was for *C-Hawk* to go to the site and drop two buoys with padded weights on the site location. The buoys were moved to each end of the orientation line. A downline from the *Anita*'s stern using a 30 pound mud anchor was rigged at one end of the site. A second line was rigged from the downline to the dive ladder on *Anita*'s port side, to help divers pull themselves up when surfacing. Every day the stern anchor lines were buoyed and released, to be retrieved by the *Anita.*

Daily excavation operations used water dredges mounted in the *C-Hawk,* which was rafted alongside and secured to *Anita.* To the extent that limited visibility allowed, sediment was examined while being hand-fanned into the dredge. Archaeologists monitored the exposed hull for signs of impact from sediment removal, but no signs were shown.

Diving conditions were difficult, with visibility at 1–2 feet, with strong tidal currents except for periods of slack tide. Divers also had to contend with a thick slurry of stinging jellyfish. Most divers wore masks that exposed only their lips, but jellyfish would wrap their tentacles around a diver's regulator and sting his lips.

Once the hull was exposed, archaeological documentation began. Video and photography were difficult because of poor visibility, except occasionally when for brief periods a clear window appeared. Still, 133 minutes of video were recorded. Because of some deterioration of stern features the stern area was not excavated. This would be done only once, when the submarine was ultimately recovered.

In the excavation the forward hatch was revealed first. The second excavation was near the stern. By the end of May 10 the forward hatch, snorkel box, cutwater, and dive planes had been exposed. The object still could not be officially identified as the *Hunley* until the last day, when the after hatch was exposed. Dredging, mapping, and examining hull encrustations, corrosion measurements, and a metal detector survey occupied the period from May 18th–27th. The next day a dredge was used to excavate a trench alongside to get an accurate measurement of the hull.

Backfilling began on May 29, using cut sections of GeoWeb—a strong plastic material—to guard against excavation attempts by outsiders. When the GeoWeb proved to be buoyant it was removed, and backfilling with sand began. Bad weather delayed the backfilling until June 3; sandbags were used on June 4 to finish the job. The site was finally stabilized to conform with the surrounding seabed and the project was finished.

In recapitulation:

First using remote sensing with a marine proton magnetometer, a RoxAnn bottom classification unit, a side-scan sonar, and a digital sub-bottom profiler, the scientists relocated the site of the *Hunley,* discovered other areas of interest, and profiled the depth of the submarine below the sediment.

Cores taken from around the site provided environmental context.

Then came several "down days" caused by bad weather. Phase Two began on May 8. This was to positively identify the submarine as the *Hunley* from several attributes unique to this vessel: the forward and after hatches with portholes and cutwaters, torpedo spar, diving planes, air box and snorkel, propeller, rudder, and external iron keel ballast. Identity was confirmed on May 17, with identification of five of the seven attributes. Dan Polly, a corrosion engineer, conducted a series of studies of the corrosion levels of the metal. All this work was made harder by high winds and heavy seas.

Once Phase Two was completed the submarine was reburied under protective silt. The site then was protected by physical barriers, electronic surveillance, and sensing devices. It was expected that analysis of the gathered data would take many months. However, some preliminary findings were available:

The *Hunley* was completely buried by harbor sediment, lying 45 degrees on its starboard side, bow to the shore. The dive planes were elevated, indicating that the boat was traveling on the surface when she was swamped, possibly in heavy seas, or that she was attempting to surface.

After the sinking she apparently became buried in the first ten years.

The hull contained much sound metal. There was little apparent damage to the one-quarter of the boat investigated: The forward face of the forward hatch coaming was fractured, possibly where there had once been a porthole.

Architecturally the *Hunley* differed from the description and sketch made by William Alexander 40 years after the boat was built, and was more like Conrad Wise Chapman's famous painting: smooth lines, converging at bow and stern, a hull 39 feet, five inches long and about three feet, 10 inches in diameter. A 4¾ inch external keel ran along the bottom of the hull. Both hatches were intact, each located nine feet from the ends. Each hatch coaming contained a small viewport on the port side, and the forward hatch coaming apparently contained one facing forward, but that one was broken. A cutwater made of a single iron plate angled forward from the forward hatch to the bow. (The aft cutwater, which at first appeared not to have existed, was indeed found separated from the boat on the seafloor. The finding took place on the final, pre-recovery excavation.)

The air box and snorkel were directly aft of the forward hatch, although only stubs of the snorkel tubes remained. Between the air box and after hatch, evenly spaced along the hull, were five pairs of flat glass deadlights, which illuminated the boat when it was on the surface. The port dive plane was six feet, 10 inches long and 8 and a half inches wide. It pivoted on a three-inch pivot pin.

No evidence was found of the spar supposedly used in the attack on the *Housatonic*. The spar remained a puzzle.

When all the studies had been made and evaluated, the final report of the expedition would be prepared and recommendations made to the South Carolina Hunley Commission and the U.S. Navy.

On August 6, 1996, the Hunley Commission and the navy signed an agreement stipulating that the *Hunley* would be the property of the United States, but the state of South Carolina would have perpetual custody. The navy and the commission agreed to cooperate on such issues as site protection, archaeological investigation, conservation, and eventual display. They also established the Hunley Oversight Committee, clearing the way for the excavation, raising, and conservation of the submarine,

Dr. William Dudley of the Naval Historical Center said that raising the *Hunley* would cost several million dollars but would be worth it to the nation.

As the scientists worked to assess the situation of the *Hunley,* the Hunley Commission began to plan ahead and in the fall agreed to solicit proposals from organizations that wanted to provide a home for the submarine when it was rehabilitated, and to exhibit it to the public.

On January 19, 1997, the Discovery Channel showed a one-hour documentary *(Rebel Beneath the Waves)* videotaped in part in Charleston. The reenactors who took part in the film donated their fee of $2000 to the recovery and preservation of the submarine; the Palmetto Battalion, the Confederate reenactors association, donated another $8000, to the recovery and reinterment of the crew's remains.

A month later the Hunley Commission announced that the hull of the submarine had been shown to be strong enough to be raised and rehabilitated. This effort was going to cost ten million dollars. Fund-raising plans were being developed by the commission and others.

On March 5, 1997, the Hunley Commission rejected Edward Lee Spence's claims to have discovered the *Hunley* and accepted Clive Cussler's claim. Cussler had funded the expedition that finally located the *Hunley.*

Spence retaliated by posting the coordinates where he claimed the *Hunley* was located on his site on the Internet.

Research continued on the findings of the exploratory expedition, particularly on the delivery of the torpedo that sank the *Housatonic.* "How was the torpedo attached to the *Hunley?*"—that was the question. Contemporary reports had it that the torpedo was attached by a wooden spar mounted at the top of the bow, but no spar was found at the site of the *Housatonic* or on the bow of the *Hunley.* And there was no evidence of fittings to mount a spar on the bow's top.

As the finishing touches were being put on the final excavations, divers found an iron rod at the bottom of the bow. It extended into the sand; how far they could not tell, but a considerable distance. The mystery of the spar was solved at last. It was an iron pipe, broken off at 17 feet in length, bolted to the boat with a simple nut and bolt. Unable to raise the *Hunley* without breaking off the spar, the archaeologists agreed to remove it. The nut came off with relative ease, but the bolt, perhaps bent in the attack on the *Housatonic,* proved more stubborn and had to be cut off.

The Hunley Commission met again on October 30 in Charleston to establish an eleemosynary corporation called Friends of the *Hunley* to raise $10 million to endow the project of raising, refurbishing, and exhibiting the submarine. The commission was also seeking a permanent home for the *Hunley.* The experts agreed that when the submarine was raised it should not be subjected to transportation strains that might damage the hull. The Patriots Point Maritime Museum near Charleston and the Charleston Museum both were interested, but in the final analysis the Charleston Museum was selected. Dr. John Brumgardt was the director.

Now came the matter of organizing the Friends of the *Hunley* to raise money. What was needed was a chairman who would put his heart into the effort.

One of the commission members, Rear Admiral William J. Schachte Jr., knew a businessman, Warren Lasch, who had recently moved from Michigan to the Charleston area. Senator McConnell had never heard of Lasch, although the man owned two trucking companies and Lasch had just recently heard of the *Hunley*. But as a businessman he was looking for a way to participate in community affairs.

"This just seemed to be the type of project that needed the skills that I've been able to develop over the years," he said. "I didn't have a strong interest in history or science but a project like this one takes vision, leadership, accounting skills, knowledge of human resources, budget analysis—almost all of the ingredients you need for successful business."

Senator McConnell offered Lasch the job. "It won't take you more than ten hours every two weeks," he said.

Ten hours every two weeks . . .

"It's been 50 hours a week for the last four years," Lasch said, recollecting that conversation.

His first accomplishment was to recruit Dr. Robert Neyland of the Naval Historical Center to organize and direct the scientific aspects. Neyland jumped in almost immediately and worked fast.

The original target for the recovery of the *Hunley* was January 2001, but fear that the vessel would be raided by pirates or damaged by accident or nature pushed the deadline to 2000. That did not leave much time for the essentials—building equipment to handle the job, building the support facility, and getting archaeologists, equipment, and staff for the operation.

But somehow Lasch and company managed. By late June preparations for the big event were almost complete. A large metal truss had been erected over the submarine. Thirty-two foam-cushioned slings, each one foot wide, had been slipped under the vessel and connected at each end of the truss.

Meanwhile the quarrel between author Clive Cussler and underwater explorer Edward Lee Spence simmered quietly and sometimes not so quietly.

Spence continued to claim that he had discovered the *Hunley* in 1970, while on a fishing trip in Charleston Harbor with friends. Cussler continued to claim that his expedition of NUMA had discovered the submarine. Spence amassed a mass of documents (more than 100 pages) to support his claim, plus a plethora of statements from editors, publishers, government officials, and adventurers that seemed to support his bona fides.

Cussler rejected all this data and offered the Hunley Commission's endorsement of his claim.

Mark Newell, only peripherally involved in this fracas, stood on the sidelines.

After Spence printed his documents on the Internet, Cussler rejected them, saying anyone could draw a line around part of the ocean—and the quarrel continued to simmer on and on and on . . .

10

RECOVERY II

CHARLESTON'S CITADEL MILITARY ACADEMY, in building a new athletic stadium in the late 1990s, discovered a graveyard in the area to be occupied by the parking lot. It was determined this graveyard contains the bodies of the five *Hunley* crewmen drowned in the first accident, under Lt. Payne. Plans were made to bring up the bodies. In the spring of 2000, the bodies were disinterred and taken to Holy Communion Church on March 24, where they lay in state from 9 A.M. until 7 P.M., when a Requiem Eucharist service was held. The next morning the bodies were taken to Magnolia Cemetery and buried near H. L. Hunley and the submariners who perished with him in the boat's second fatal accident.

Now all the crewmen of the *Hunley* had been accounted for except the members of the final crew that sank the *Housatonic*. When the submarine was raised and the bodies brought out, they, too, would given all honors and military burial, and their *Hunley* adventure would be ended.

As the scientists labored to prepare the *Hunley* for its journey to land, the controversy erupted again, as a citizen asked the question on the Web:

Who discovered the *Hunley*?

Dr. Newell reentered the fray because he had severed his connection with the South Carolina Institute of Archaeology and Anthropology and no longer felt constrained to keep quiet. Freed of his SCIAA afiliation, Newell gave full credence to Edward Lee Spence's claim that he had discovered the boat quite by accident in 1970 on a fishing trip with friends. And this time the coordinates were there:

32 degrees 43 minutes 08.25 seconds north latitude,
79 degrees 46 minutes 29.33 seconds west longitude.

These coordinates were accurate. They had been given by Cussler's people to the state Hunley Commission and locked away by that commission for five years until revealed by a newspaperman in a series of articles for South Carolina newspapers.

Here are Spence's own words describing the positioning of the coordinates:

A comparison of those coordinates with the position Spence had plotted in his annotated chart in the chapter about his discovery in his 1995 book *The Treasures of the Confederate Coast* (published just three months before Cussler's claim) shows an error of about 42 meters, which is "coincidentally" the same as the error of 42 meters perceived error for the position reported by NUMA, which may be another indication that NUMA used his published map.

To understand Spence's amazing degree of accuracy, it should be noted that this is a mere 0.02 inch plotting error on the standard 1:80,000 scale navigational chart of the area. (NOAA 11521—Charleston Harbor and approaches) That is not even the width of a pencil dot. Even more amazing is that Spence's was plotted from bearings taken aboard a rocking boat with a sextant and handheld magnetic compass to floating channel buoys 1,200 yards away and to the Sullivan's Island and Morris Island lighthouses, which were over 4 & 5 miles away respectively. The now standard GPS (Global Positioning System) did not exist in the 1970s when Spence plotted and reported his position for the *Hunley*, and even now GPS still has "guaranteed" accuracy of no more than 100 meters. The government's extremely precise coordinates were obtained with the latest in satellite positioning technology combined with onshore base stations. A revised plot, base on notes made by Spence circa 1979, shows his position was actually less than five feet off by longitude.

Spence has put together computer overlays of maps to show that the State's official coordinates closely match not only the map shown in his 1995 book, but also the center point of an earlier map he filed with the United States Army Corps of Engineers and the US Navy when he was seeking permission to salvage the *Hunley* in 1974.

The facts clearly are on Spence's side. Among those agreeing with Spence are Mark Newell and Claude Petrone.

Dr. Newell is a former underwater archaeologist with the South Carolina Institute of Archaeology and Anthropology and was the originator and director of the *Hunley* search project that Cussler helped fund. Dr. Newell told Spence that what his project's divers actually did was to "rediscover" the *Hunley*.

That is quite an endorsement since it comes from the man listed in Cussler's original 1995 press release as the project's director. Dr. Newell's confirmation of my discovery proves that he is an honest and honorable man. By supporting me he is walking away from credit that he could have claimed for his own. But that would have been wrong. I admire him for his integrity.

Petrone, retired Chief of Special Photographic Projects for the *National Geographic* magazine, first reviewed Spence's evidence in 1990 and is personally convinced Spence discovered the *Hunley*.

Spence also points out that on September 14, 1995, he donated his rights to the *Hunley* to the State of South Carolina at the request of Hunley Commission chairman Senator Glenn McConnell. The donation document was signed by South Carolina Attorney General Charles M. Condon, who had listened to Spence's sworn statement before the commission and had previously reviewed Spence's written account and other evidence supporting his claim. On September 20, 1995 Condon wrote Spence, "Let me express my sincere appreciation and profound gratitude for your generous and historic donation to the State of your rights to the submarine *HL Hunley*." Two months later South Carolina Governor David M. Beasley wrote Spence, "Your work in discovering *Hunley* is of great significance. South Carolina is indebted to you for the wonderful contribution you have made to archaeology."

Chris Amer, a deputy state archaeologist with SCIAA, wrote Spence on February 2, 1996 stating that if the *Hunley*'s coordinates were within the circular area indicated on the 1980 Admiralty Case document, "Dr. Leader and I will agree that you saw and located the submarine prior to NUMA."

Spence can now prove that the *Hunley*'s official coordinates are within the circular area. . . .

The investigation of the *Hunley* site had shown the scientists that the hull of the submarine was sound and there would be minimal danger involved in lifting it, so in the spring and summer of 2000 preparations were made for the lift from the bottom. By midsummer they were complete. Divers cleared the silt from around the submarine and then strapped it tightly along its entire length to reduce the strain on any one part of the hull. At the Charleston Museum a holding tank was built and filled with seawater at a temperature slightly above freezing.

Then the recovery program hit a snag.

They had anticipated recovering the submarine with a floating barge crane, but when they tried they found it did not work with any degree of certainty. It was unable to lift the submarine fast enough to suit the scientists.

The ocean swells in the area rise and fall an average of two feet every ten or twelve seconds, the crane lifts at 12 to 14 feet per minute or about two feet every ten seconds, and since the crane could not lift the submarine more than two feet in the first ten seconds, any swell of more than two feet would smash the submarine back onto the ocean floor. The *Hunley* was too precious to risk the possible damage. The floating barge crane was out of the question. What was needed was a fixed-leg crane. The only one they could find that could do the job was the *Carlissa B,* which was in the Dominican Republic, not available, and would not be until hurricane season when clearly it would be too dangerous to attempt the recovery.

Fortunately the owners of the *Carlissa B* came to the rescue in time and sent the *Carlissa B,* and crews to man it, up to Charleston.

As they waited for the crane to arrive the scientists began to grow restless. The *Hunley* could be seen just below the surface, surrounded by its cagelike structure, suspended in its sling. But at the eleventh hour the crane came. On August 8 a crowd of small craft milled about the *Hunley* site, awaiting the recovery; there were several delays. But just after 8:30 in the morning the tall crane aboard the barge began to move. Shortly afterward the *Hunley* emerged, safe in its cradle, and was hoisted aboard the barge and into its tank. The crowd cheered; the small boats raced around.

The Hunley *resurfaces, August 8, 2000. Suspended by its supporting truss, the submarine is being placed on the barge in the foreground for transport to the conservation facility in Charleston.* Naval Historical Center photograph by Barbara Voulgaris.

The crowd cheered more and applauded. Warren Lasch and Senator McConnell embraced. Everyone congratulated everyone else, and Dr. Robert Neyland was held in the midst of an admiring crowd.

Not to be upstaged, Clive Cussler leaped overboard from his boat and splashed around in the water.

Mass confusion broke out as boats jockeyed for position. The triumphal voyage back to Charleston was about to begin, and this was the submarine's escort. People waved and shouted as the boats passed Fort Sumter, the

Bow view of the Hunley *shortly after recovery, showing the diving planes.* Courtesy Friends of the *Hunley.*

jetties, and moved into the harbor. As they passed the battery, the aircraft carrier *Yorktown* fired a signal gun.

Traffic was held up on the Cooper River Bridge, and people got out of their cars and lined the bridge rail.

Michael Trouche of Charleston's TV Channel 5 accompanied the procession and gave commentary on historical and current events. Photographer David McCabe of Charleston recorded the event, from the raising of the submarine to its delivery in Charleston. Minutes before the procession passed by Magnolia Cemetery, he was there to take pictures, greeted by a reenactor who was playing the role of guard. As the procession went by the guard presented arms to the passing crew, then turned and presented arms to the *Hunley*'s second crew in their graves, then left.

Soon the procession reached the Warren Lasch Conservation Center, where the *Hunley* was carefully lifted by another crane and moved toward her new home, escorted by reenactors who mounted a color guard with the flags of the United States and the second national flag of the Confederacy, and the Charleston Naval Squadron.

Inside the museum the reenactors meandered around; Clive Cussler's crew waited for cameras to flash and bodies to move about. A bugler played Taps.

The *Hunley* had arrived home, safe and sound. Now the work of conservation could begin.

11

CONSERVING
THE *HUNLEY*

IN MARINE ARCHAEOLOGY, *conservation* means to preserve an object. The majority of objects found on the ocean floor need to be preserved with special chemicals. If this is not done quickly and properly, the artifacts will deteriorate.

When conservators receive an artifact they usually follow a four-step procedure:

1. *Documentation.*
   Conservators document objects by videotaping, photographing, and drawing them.
2. *Analysis.*
   Researchers sometimes X ray objects if they are covered with concretion. Concretion is made up of grains of sand, shells, particles of coral, and sea plants. This begins to build up on objects beneath the sea. Metal objects start immediately to corrode. Soon the corrosion

is accompanied by accretion of a hard shell—concretion. Elimination of concretion is a painstaking and tedious operation. Conservators X ray the object first. They must determine the exact shape underneath the outer coating. After determining the fragility of the artifact, the conservator uses special tools to free the object of the concretion. The amount of concretion built up depends on the location of the object under the sea and the length of time it was submerged.

3. *Cleaning.*

When removed from the sea, artifacts contain salt (sodium chloride). Nautical archaeologist Donny Hamilton, director of the conservation laboratory at Texas A and M University, says: "Artifacts from a marine environment are saturated with salts that must be removed. In addition the saltwater environment accelerates corrosion of many metal objects. If the salts are not removed in time, the artifacts deteriorate and become useless as museum specimens."

The salinity content varies greatly from ocean to ocean. As a rule: the less salt, the less destruction. For example, artifacts from the 17th century Swedish warship *Vasa,* raised in Stockholm in 1961, were remarkably well preserved because of the low salt content of the Baltic Sea.

But generally, if the object is left untreated, the salt reacting with the air will cause the object to crumble away.

4. *Stabilization.*

Conservators stabilize artifacts to protect them against a bad reaction when removed from seawater. One method is electrolysis. Electrolysis is a time-consuming process that draws salt out of the metal by running an electrical current through the object. The more salt, the more time it takes. Objects are treated according to their makeup; for example, porcelain, bronze, and wood are all treated differently.

The conservation process stabilizes the object by use of special chemicals and tools. Cannon, for example, are usually stored in top water with additional chemicals added to prevent further corrosion.

As the *Hunley* was brought to shore for the first time in nearly a century and a half, the scientists were already working on her conservation. For several years they had been studying the experience of other nations in this field, particularly the restoration of the Viking ships by Norway, the warship *Vasa* by Sweden, and the Tudor warship *Mary Rose* by England. They knew that the *Hunley* was equal, if not superior, in importance to these legendary finds.

In the year 1880 farmers in Sandar, Norway, began digging in what was known as The King's Mound, a hillock five meters high and 43 meters in diameter, located on the Gokstad farm. They suspected they knew what they were looking for—a Viking grave. Norsemen of old honored their chieftains by ritual burial in the ships they sailed.

Antiquary Nicolay Nicolaysen joined the hunt, and since he was the only one who had any concept of archaeology, he was soon running the show. When the stern of ship was unearthed in the mound of blue clay and sand, it became apparent that an important find had been made.

The mound is a good long way (400 meters) from the mouth of any of the fjords. The Vikings had hauled the ship up the Hasle River, which runs close to the mound.

The excavation of the ship took several months. When the Gokstad ship was unearthed it turned out to be whole and in surprisingly good condition. The ship was built in about the year 890 A.D. and the tomb was put in place sometime between 900 and 905 A.D. It was transported by barge to Oslo and restored to its original state, then put on display at the Viking Ships Museum near Oslo.

In the autumn of 1997, Danish dredgers at Roskilde unearthed a Viking longship while deepening the harbor to expand it for the museum's fleet of historic ship replicas. Archaeologists were called in and identified the vessel. According to the head of the museum the longship must have sunk in a storm centuries ago and then been covered by silt. Tree ring dating of the oak planking put its age at nearly 1000 years. With its formidable length of

35 meters the longship proved finally that the ships described in Norse sagas were real and not the myths the doubters claimed them to be. These longships were vital in seaborne raiding; fleets of them attacked coasts from Northumberland to North Africa, carried pioneers to the British Isles and to Normandy, and made the Vikings the dominant sea power in Europe from around 800 to 1100, the Viking era.

Longships had been very much in the minds of Danish archaeologists since 1935, when the remains of one were discovered at Ladby. Actual timbers of a longship were found in a burial mound on the German border in 1953, and this sparked the interest of Ole Crumlin Pederson, an 18-year-old who began to dive for sunken Viking ships. Between 1957 and 1962 he led others in discovery of two longships and three other Viking ships from a channel near Skyuldev, where they had been sunk in the 11th century to create a barricade by some townsfolk against invaders.

In 1979 Crumlin Pederson discovered the Hedeby longship; it had been deliberately set afire as an offensive weapon in an attack on Hedeby in about 1000.

The *Vasa* was a battle galleon built in 1628 for the king of Sweden, Gustavus Adolphus, to his own specifications. It was the greatest ship of her time, part of his fleet of warships that patrolled the Baltic Sea.

She was what is called "skeleton built," with two gun decks that housed 64 bronze cannon. Her construction was mainly of northern oak, a very strong wood. It is said that her timber took a forest of 40 acres. The timbers of the bow were steamed to curve them and fixed, and the close-set ribs were clad with heavy timber walls, a masterpiece of triple-laminated oak 1.8 inches (6 cm) thick. A web of masts and spars rose high above the deck; the topgallant on the mainmast was 190 feet high. The rudder was more than 30 feet tall.

On August 10, 1628, the *Vasa* set sail on her maiden voyage in a light breeze blowing from the southwest. Her sails were not gotten up until the ship reached Sodermalm, in the southern outskirts of the harbor. Majestically, as befitted such a large ship, she fired a salute upon leaving harbor. Then a sudden squall sprang up and she was caught by a strong gust of wind, while her gunports were still open. She listed heavily to port, the water rushed in through the open gunports, and . . .

GURGLE!

GURGLE!

GURGLE!

She sank in a few moments to the bottom, 100 feet below the surface and only about 100 yards from shore, in water so clear you could see her lying there below.

The first attempt to salvage her came shortly after a memorial service held for her drowned victims. Ian

Bulmer, the royal engineer, succeeded in setting her on an even keel, because her mainmast stuck up out of the water. But his further efforts were unsuccessful. The ship settled in the muddy bottom of Stockholm Harbor.

The *Vasa* was abandoned and soon forgotten, with no trace of her or her location.

Early in the 1950s Anders Franzen, a treasure hunter in his twenties, began looking for buried treasure among the islands of Stockholm Harbor. He talked with fishermen and sailors, used sounding devices, dragnets, and a small motor launch. He heard a fable about the *Vasa* from his father and began to study old records. Soon he considered himself to be a marine archaeologist. He discovered that the water in which the *Vasa* was assumed to have sunk was fresh to brackish because the great lake of Malaren passes through Stockholm there. Using a core sampler in an area near the Stockholm Navy Yard, one day in August 1956 he brought up a black oak core. He informed the Swedish navy, whose chief diver went down and claimed the *Vasa* for the Crown. He found her upright, but buried to the original waterline in mud and clay.

A *Vasa* committee was established and decided to salvage the ship by raising her to the surface. This was a risky procedure, because (as was a concern with the *Hunley*) she might collapse in the process. But as one of the foremost marine archaeologists wrote later, "The real significance of the *Vasa* discovery lay in the fact that no record of naval architecture exist for the first half of the seventeenth century."

Here was a cross section of life containing antiquities that had been preserved by the sea. She was also an example of shipbuilding and naval architecture that was little known and would therefore be of great value.

Five navy divers undertook the perilous job of drilling tunnels beneath the *Vasa*'s keel. Six tunnels were called for, with cables to be strung through them and then used to raise the ship via two pontoons. The tunnel construction took almost a year, three tunnels from each side of the ship.

The two pontoons were attached to the ship by cables. After they had lifted her from the mud, they swung her around and headed slowly for Kastellhomen, where she was grounded in sheltered water. Then she was moved again to even more sheltered water, still 50 feet below the surface. She was now ready to be raised in one piece. The plan was to repair her under water, then float her up so she could enter the dock on her own keel.

At 9:03 on the morning of April 24, 1961, the *Vasa* came to the surface, first a piece of black oak, then two rows of bulwark stanchions. The damaged superstructure had finally come into view. Supported by its pontoons the ship was moved into shallower water, where a special pump was used to take out water faster than it was leaking into her. After 333 years submerged, she began to rise.

Submersible pumps kept her afloat in the harbor and sprayed her steadily with water for two weeks while frogmen corked more leaks under water.

The last 100 yards into the dry dock the *Vasa* had to make on her own keel, for there was no room for the pontoons. She was really afloat now, if listing a bit to port.

As one official wrote, "The six-year-long adventure of winning back the *Vasa* was over."

Now the work of restoration and preservation could begin.

The fact was that the *Vasa* had been well preserved under water. This made it not too difficult a task to resurrect her. On June 17, 1961, surrounded by a new pontoon whose center was covered over with concrete frames, the *Vasa* left Beckholm Dock and slowly crossed the harbor to reach a sheltered spot near Skansen Park. And then the public was let in to see her, after years of following her through the media.

The conservators set to work with special equipment, high-precision tools, separators, sprinklers, several different laboratories, and even a big electric gantry.

She was put into a special pontoon 60 yards long and 23 yards wide, moved over to the shipyard and then to land near Skansen Park, and a museum was created to house her artifacts. There, today, Stockholmers and visitors can view the magnificent ship and ponder the greatness of Sweden in her day of glory.

The English warship *Mary Rose* is the only 16th century warship on display anywhere in the world. She was built at the Royal Dockyard in Portsmouth for the Royal Navy, launched in 1510, and served until she foundered during the Battle of Spithead against the French fleet on July 18, 1545, and sank off Southsea Castle. There she remained, unremarked, until 1965 when the search for the wreck began. This was at the inspiration of Alexander McKee. In conjunction with the Southsea branch of the British SubAqua Club, he began a project—"Solent Ships"—to examine a number of wrecks in the Solent. But what he really wanted was to find the *Mary Rose.*

When ordinary search techniques proved useless, he heard of the development of a sidescan sonar, and in collaboration with Professor Harold Edgerton of MIT and John Mills of the British firm of EG & G, he began seeking the wreck site. In 1967 they discovered something strange in the seabed: a large oval-shaped mound headed toward no-man's-land. The protuberances gave the impression of a flattened letter *W,* exceedingly angular and, oddly, smaller at the ends than in the middle.

"Oh, ho," said McKee.

They had discovered the *Mary Rose,* which today can be seen in Portsmouth, England.

When the discovery of the *Hunley* was confirmed, the scientists got to work. The first step was to find out what they had. Salinity, pH, Eh, conductivity, oxygen, and water temperature had to be measured with special instruments. An extensive microbiological study was begun by Dr. Pam Morris of the Fort Johnson Marine Biomedicine and Environment Agency. When completed it would give a picture of the bacterial communities around the submarine. Corrosion measurements were made by a team under Paul Mardikian and Steve West of Orion Research. The *Hunley* had been in the water for so long that the attempt to raise her might raise the rate of corrosion so high as to destroy the hull. At 90°F the rate of corrosion would be increased 7500 times. Fortunately an inspection of the vessel revealed not a single crack in the hull.

In July 1999, seeking information about the *Hunley,* the scientists went back to the wreck of the *Housatonic,* which had lain undisturbed for ninety years. They wanted to establish the extent and orientation of the wreck, determine where the ship had been hit by the *Hunley's* torpedo and how much damage was sustained, and gather such artifacts as remained.

This was not an easy task, for (as noted) the *Housatonic* wreck had been dynamited years after the Civil War to reduce its menace to navigation. After the boilers were removed, very little of the wreck remained above the sediment line.

But when divers got to work they found that the lower hull of the *Housatonic* was largely intact, except for the starboard stern, which was the area of impact of the torpedo.

About 100 artifacts were raised, including a pistol, leather shoes, bits of copper and brass chain, an iron strap, and several other items. All were taken to the Naval Historical Center for conservation, and were slated to be exhibited with *Hunley* in the Charleston Museum and in the Navy Museum in Washington.

After five years of quarreling among federal and state officials over jurisdiction and such matters, the *Hunley* was recovered on August 8, 2000. She was brought ashore at the old U.S. Navy base in North Charleston, and transferred from the barge to a tank of fresh water, 55′×1′×9′ specially built in a warehouse there for stabilization. The water was refrigerated to 50°F over a three-day period in order to remove fungus and algae and cut down the rate of corrosion.

For some time the scientists contented themselves with exterior examination of the submarine. Thus they discovered a skylight that had never appeared in any drawings or specifications, located on top of the front hatch.

Since no oxygen had entered the hull during the recovery process, they were not under any constraints of immediacy to open the hull. And they were sensitive to the fact that the *Hunley* was also, in effect, a tomb.

"The project can safely wait until January when it can proceed uninterruptedly to handle, in the most professional way, the removal of all remains from the submarine," said Hunley Commission chairman Glenn McConnell.

While waiting they toyed with different approaches—whether to remove a conning tower or panels of the hull. They finally opted to remove panels. First they drained the water out of the tank, hosed off the *Hunley,* and, taking off a few slings, used a laser to make a three-dimensional map of the hull. For the first time they had precise measurements of the submarine.

They also discovered a starboard-side viewing port on the front conning tower, to match one on the port side found earlier.

The interior of the submarine had been painted white. The hole in the starboard side appeared not to have been made in the attack on the *Housatonic,* but by an anchor dragging across the hull before the submarine was covered by silt.

Attempts to X ray the interior were unsuccessful; silt and sand had become so tightly packed that clear images could not be obtained.

On January 22, 2001, preliminary excavation began on an existing hole in the stern ballast tank. On February 14 the archaeologists finished drilling the last of 94 rivets holding one hull plate. On February 16 the first hull plate was removed, in a three-hour operation. (Eventually they removed four plates.) The submarine was found to be filled with very fine sediment with the consistency of clay.

On March 2 the excavation began on the interior. During the first week the work was confined to removing buckets of sediment—20 buckets from the submarine's upper section. The sediment was sifted through a series of three screens, and the scientists found only bits of coal and wood and some seashells.

No one had expected the submarine to reveal her secrets easily. She had so far resisted even the most sophisticated recovery equipment. On March 15 archaeologist Mike Scafuri saw the edge of a wooden plank on the port side of the submarine. The first personal artifacts—two encrusted buttons—were found on the plank.

Four days later they found a corked bottle.

The first human remains were found on March 21— the right-side rib bones of one *Hunley* crewman. The bones were studied and it was discovered that this crewman had a bad back, a herniated spinal disk. Archaeologists also found a small piece of cloth.

On March 27 the leg bones of a second sailor were discovered. On March 30 the remains of the third crewman were uncovered. On April 2 the bones of the fourth crewman were discovered, and by April 6 they had discovered partial remains of six of the crew members. On April 10 the team announced the discovery of a shoe and more buttons, a lead pencil, a tin canteen, and a wooden pipe. On

April 13 they found the first skull, and on April 16 they announced that they had found the remains of all the crew except Lt. Dixon.

On April 24 the archaeologists announced that one of the crewmen had a filling in a tooth. They also found another pipe and a sewing kit. On April 27 they announced that they had found one of the most unusual findings yet: a Union dogtag belonging to a Union soldier, Ezra Chamberlin. This find stirred up waves of speculation. Could one of the crewmen have been a Yankee deserter who embraced the Confederacy? Or a prisoner forced to join the crew? Finally a more likely scenario emerged: The dogtag was a battlefield souvenir, most likely taken by Cpl. Carlson, one of the documented crewmen. Chamberlin, from Connecticut, was apparently killed on July 11, 1863, in the Battle of Fort Wagner near Charleston.

It was backbreaking work of the most tedious sort. There was no room for free movement. Archaeologist Paul Mardikian said it was much harder than excavating a tomb. You could open a tomb, but with the *Hunley* they were severely cramped. Sometimes they worked on their knees. Sometimes they had to lie on their sides, sometimes on their backs. Mardikian spent 15 hours carefully removing a candle that had lit the submarine during the last hours of its final voyage.

Every day began with preparing the submarine for recovery work. This meant emptying the freshwater tank in which the *Hunley* was immersed. Every evening they had to refill the water tank. If the *Hunley* dried up, then the submarine and its artifacts would disappear in corrosion. The vessel was so permeated with salt that it would crumble if dried out. The archaeologists estimated it would take about ten years to leach all the salt out of the submarine.

On April 30 the archaeologists announced discovery of more personal items—two pocketknives and a slouch hat. On May 10 they announced the finding of brain tissue inside six of the recovered skulls. In the second week of May they removed an iron plate and opened the forward compartment of the submarine. On May 21 they found the remains of Lt. Dixon as well as the signal lantern, the legendary "blue light" that he used to signal Battery Marshall that the *Hunley* had succeeded in sinking the *Housatonic.*

With summer coming, they began to work double shifts, and in the forward compartment Dixon's effects began to emerge. But his clothing was so fragile that they had to cut the sediment into sections and lift it out of the submarine. Outside they had the space and equipment to separate the cloth from the mud.

Senior archaeologist Maria Jacobsen, nicknamed "Goldfinger" because of her penchant for finding gold objects, discovered the $20 gold piece that saved Dixon's leg in the Battle of Shiloh and later was his good-luck charm. Ms. Jacobsen had joined the team, suspending work on her doctoral dissertation. "I haven't been in my office for four months," she said early in May. "I'm in that tank from eight o'clock in the morning until ten o'clock at night. One of the things the team will have soon, is that we will get a trip to a spa." She was working on her back in the muck—positioned thus because the space was narrow and she was the smallest member of the archaeological team—when she found the gold piece. Two other members of the team were lifting a sediment block; Jacobsen slid her hand under the plate and and felt something hard. The gold piece had been in Dixon's left trouser pocket.

The recovery was never easy. "She defied our gamma rays, she defied our probes, she popped drill bits back at us, she defied the jaws of time," McConnell said. "Now reluctantly she is giving up her story. The story has been worth the wait."

"The entire excavation has been one surprise after another," said Warren Lasch:

You'll be at the sifter, and you'll find a long blond hair or red hair, or you'll find an eyelash. You'll find pieces of textile and you'll see a sleeve actually still wrapped around the bones of an arm.

On the bench where they sat, there was a little semicircular cutout where the man sat, working the pump for the rear ballast tank, and you just knew that after he hit his knuckles on that bench twenty or thirty times he said "We'll have to fix this." And he fixed it with that little cutout. There's so much history here and so much science here but when you actually start working, you see that these people were very human.

On May 25 the archaeologists stopped for a break because they were exhausted and Dr. Neyland had several commitments in the summer months. They planned to get back to work on the *Hunley* in September.

After Labor Day the scientific work was resumed. But the summer was not without its excitement.

Several new facts emerged. The *Hunley* had not carried a crew of nine on her last voyage, but a crew of only eight men, including the skipper. Eight skeletons were found, and in fact eight may have been the full crew. Seven cranking stations were all that emerged. A theory as to the cause of the *Hunley*'s sinking was called into question; the submarine didn't sink because of small-arms fire from the *Housatonic* that shot out the glass in the front conning tower and may have killed or wounded Lt. Dixon, causing consternation among the crew. Dixon's remains, at least from initial X ray, showed no wounds. In fact, there was no evidence of any excitement down below. The bodies were found all at their posts, evidently dead from anoxia, oxygen deprivation. The boat had not filled with water, as in the two previous sinkings. Stalactites were discovered hanging from the submarine's roof, formed of carbonite, caused by water dripping for a long time. So the water that filled the boat came later, long after the sinking and death of the crew.

In addition, a previously unknown and undocumented air bellows was found, with a system of hoses to distribute fresh air. Speculation continues that the bellows was a late improvement to the *Hunley,* since it is never mentioned by McClintock, Alexander, or any of the other *Hunley* designers or witnesses who left written records.

There is also surprise over how the *Hunley* began. Lt. Alexander had described the *Hunley* as built from a boiler, with sections added. Yet the construction of the *Hunley* clearly shows a more elegant construction, consisting of a skeleton frame to which iron plates were attached.

Summer 2001 also brought new controversy: emergence of a new claim by the Point Pleasant Museum to house the *Hunley* permanently. The Point Pleasant Museum had been nosed out in the competition by the Charleston Museum to house the submarine across the Cooper River. But Charleston mayor Joseph P. Riley had taken a stand against display of the Confederate battle flag in connection with the *Hunley,* and officials of the South

Carolina chapter of the Sons of Confederate Veterans claimed that this stand disqualified Charleston from displaying the *Hunley*.

"The *Hunley* represents the things we've always talked about, the regular citizen-soldier willing to die for the defense of the homeland," said Gene Hogan, chairman of the SCV Heritage Committee.

On June 14 the Patriot's Point Development Authority offered a million dollars if state officials would choose Patriot's Point for the permanent display. Previously the authority had offered land for a future museum. Mount Pleasant mayor Harry Hallman had offered a $4 million hospitality tax to bring the submarine across the river.

For the *Hunley* will be big business: It is expected to become the state's prime tourist attraction.

"It's a fascinating artifact and it's something important to the history of South Carolina. And it's going to be a moneymaker," Hogan added. "It would be hypocritical of Riley to profit off the submarine after criticizing the Confederate battle flag."

To which Mayor Riley responded that he did not oppose all displays of Confederate battle flags, but had opposed the battle flag on the statehouse because it had been adopted by some groups as a symbol of hate, and that the statehouse and public agreed with him.

On Thursday, August 16, Edward Lee Spence gave evidence that he had not given up on his campaign to be acknowledged as the discoverer of the *Hunley* in 1970. He told a crowd of 60 people at Charleston's Karpeles Manuscript Library Museum that he would continue his fight for recognition. He had been invited to speak by the Charleston Historical Society. The Hunley Commission had long accepted author Clive Cussler's claim that a team of his National Underwater and Marine Agency had discovered the submarine. Spence said he was not seeking glory, but only truth.

So the controversy continued.

On September 6 the Friends of the *Hunley* announced extension of their tours of the Warren Lasch Conservation Center through the end of the year. It had been anticipated that the tours would end after Labor Day because of the resumption of archaeological work on the submarine, but Chairman Warren Lasch said tours would resume on September 22 and run through the end of the year. Visitors could see the submarine as she was undergoing the phases of excavation.

By September 29, 80 percent of the crew compartment had been cleared of silt, although the front and rear bulkheads had not; some of the diving controls were also still covered, as well as the space under the wooden bench on which the crew sat to turn the cranks. The archaeologists hoped to find a treasure trove beneath the bench, the most likely spot for stowage of personal items.

The scientists were still wondering what had caused the submarine's demise. No "smoking gun" had yet been discovered, no readable clues to the cause of the tragedy.

Scientific director Robert Neyland said the final phase of excavation should be completed by Christmastime, but warned that this did not mean they would have all the answers to such questions.

Hunley Commission chairman Glenn McConnell said he expected a recommendation as to the permanent home of the *Hunley* to be made by February.

In October Clive Cussler filed a lawsuit in federal court against Edward Lee Spence, charging defamation of character. Cussler asked for a jury trial.

"It's about bragging rights," one lawyer said, "but they're important bragging rights."

The suit alleged that Spence defamed the NUMA achievement in finding the submarine, and damaged the reputation of the three divers who claimed to have found it. The suit also charged that Spence used the Internet, the media, and public statements to attack NUMA as incompetent, which damaged the group's ability to conduct future searches.

Spence welcomed the suit, and said he expected to file a countersuit to set the record straight.

On October 12 archaeologists excavated a flywheel designed to act as a brake on the propeller. "Again this shows us how far ahead of their time were the engineers who designed and built the *Hunley*," said Robert Neyland. "This complex system graphically demonstrates the advanced technology of *Hunley* and dispels any notion that it was a primitive submarine fashioned from a boiler."

Added Senator Glenn McConnell, "It further emphasizes the case for the final exhibit to concentrate part of its focus on the sciences and technologies employed in designing and building a craft 50 years ahead of its time."

In mid-October the archaeologists predicted that the burial of the *Hunley* crew members would not occur until 2003, for they would need two years to examine bones for injuries that may give clues. They also planned forensic examinations of the eight skulls found, to re-create the facial construction of each man.

The Hunley Project had been delayed by the September 11 terrorist attacks on Washington and New York. Some of the forensics experts who were going to conduct DNA testing became occupied with the victims of the Pentagon and World Trade Center attacks.

On October 20 the archaeologists began digging in the forward conning tower, hoping to find evidence of the reason for the sinking. Glass shards would indicate damage before the sinking. Metal in the sediment would mean that the damage likely occurred long after the submarine went down. Objects on the deck would indicate that the damage occurred before the submarine filled with silt. As of this date they have found no glass or iron, but only a portion of the sediment has been removed. The diggers have uncovered more of the after ballast tank and seacock and the bench that the crew sat on, mounted on the port side of the hull, with support by a number of brackets. Four canteens were found here, bringing the total to seven. They have also found three of the bolts that held the submarine's keel ballast, indicating that an attempt was made to drop the ballast and lighten the boat.

Dr. Robert Neyland said the excavation would continue through the autumn; there remained a meter of sediment to be removed to reach the forward controls, where Lt. Dixon steered the submarine.

On October 26 archaeologists announced the continuing excavation of the forward section of the central compartment. The sediment had been fully documented and removed, and the excavators were approaching the forward bulkhead. Forward of the conning tower they located a curved pipe that was connected to the port side of the hull. It could have been the intake valve for the forward seacock.

Excavation also continued in the after section of the central compartment. The team had exposed more of the mechanism around the propulsion gears and flywheel as well as the after pump assembly and after seacock. The propulsion gears connected to the propeller assembly by a chain that was still in place.

Archaeologists also reached the stern and located the after bulkhead, which was open, some 43 cm behind the after conning tower.

This discovery confirms historical recollections that the flood compartments were not sealed off from the crew compartment, but were open. With the otherwise incredibly advanced engineering seen in the *Hunley,* it raises the question of why they left it that way. They had developed the ability to use glass ports and could have sealed it off but still have maintained the ability to see within it.

If the submarine was rocked by the explosion of the *Housatonic*'s boiler, or run over by one of the ships assembling around the sunken *Housatonic,* any substantial tilting of the submarine could have resulted in water pouring out of the flood tanks and into the crew compartment, creating an imbalance and robbing the submarine of its near-positive buoyancy. This might have left it stranded under the surface, unable to purge the water and regain its surface position. With a limited amount of air, conditions would be ripe for anoxia, a quick loss of oxygen, resulting in unconsciousness. Unable to come to the surface, the submarine would have been able to rely only on its snorkels. It could skim along under the surface to gather air, but the crew would possibly be using more air than they could bring in, thus sealing their fate.

Perhaps that is what happened, and the cause of the deaths of the eight-man crew. At this juncture it seems the most likely solution to the riddle.

On November 16 the archaeologists announced the finding and removal of a waterlogged box containing the submarine's compass. Attached to the box was a gimbel, or pivoting ring, which allowed the compass to swing freely and stabilize at a level position.

The excavations also uncovered a vertical steering rod 70 centimeters in front of the submarine hinged at the bottom to uncovered connections, leading back to a pipe that runs down the side of the submarine underneath the crew compartment to the stern. This vertical steering rod, like an airplane joystick, could move in two directions, from port to starboard. It seems to be part of a steering mechanism of rods and cables to connect the rudder, while placing it out of the crew's way. "Simple and elegant," archaeologist Maria Jacobsen called it.

The search for the answer to why the *Hunley* sank now moved to the blocks of sediment removed from the submarine and preserved in the laboratory for further study.

In announcing a new tour schedule in December, Warren Lasch also announced the continuing search for a permanent home for the *Hunley*. The original award of the valuable property to the Charleston Museum had been vacated, and the competition opened to other entities. By December this had evolved down to three serious contenders, the Charleston Museum, North Charleston, and Point Pleasant.

Senator McConnell announced that detailed plans from the three would be taken. "We are this week sending out guidelines for proposals asking the entities to address several points, to allow a decision on the permanent home of the *Hunley* Maritime Exhibit. These proposals ask for information about how the government entity would handle parking, exhibition, location, and general operation, how future conservation would be handled, and how revenues would be handled. This information should help make the February date for decision a reality."

North Charleston had become a serious contender in November, with a move joining the Noisette Company to help draft its proposal to house the *Hunley*. Noisette is made up of some of the nation's leading urban planners. It is leading the $1 billion development of the former Charleston Navy Base and surrounding neighborhoods. Mayor Keith Summey said he hoped Noisette's expertise would give North Charleston the edge in the struggle. The North Charleston plan is to transform the northern end of the former base into a waterfront park.

"We think the *Hunley* will be a major draw for the city, much as the aquarium is for Charleston," the mayor said.

The *Hunley* could be the crown jewel of a 3000 acre redevelopment program that ranges from building a waterfront to new commercial and residential development.

For the *Hunley* is big bucks—already a cash cow.

Mount Pleasant and Charleston were both eager to stay in the race and doing their best to win it for themselves. Charleston officials are talking about putting the *Hunley* near the aquarium.

Mt. Pleasant is talking about building a $5 million museum to house the submarine at Patriot's Point.

It is likely to become the state of South Carolina's leading tourist attraction when it goes on public display later in this decade. Senator McConnell expects it to draw at least a million people a year in the beginning and to average 500,000 over a few years, pumping millions of dollars into the state's economy.

"The *Hunley* seems to have captured the imagination of the world," McConnell said. "Visitors from all 50 states and five continents have become 'Hunleytized.'"

With only word-of-mouth advertising, more than 70,000 visitors have visited the Warren Lasch Conservation Laboratory since the *Hunley* arrived in August 2000.

The Hunley Commission hopes to expand the draw by building a 60,000 square-foot Civil War maritime museum to house the submarine, telling the entire story of the war at sea.

No other place in the nation can compete with this because it rolls together the story of American technology, patriotism, and workmanship along with the love story between Commander Dixon and his sweetheart Queenie Bennett.

"It's a message that reverberates around the world," McConnell claimed.

He has envisioned that the *Hunley* museum will include a virtual-reality tour of life aboard the vessel, facial re-creations of all the submarine's crewmen, and thousands of wartime artifacts relating to the war at sea.

Besides that the museum will take on an expanded level as a research and work center for artifact preservation at the corporate, technological, and academic levels. "South Carolina will become the cutting edge for underwater archaeological preservation."

Yet when all the facts are in, when the *Hunley* has been scrubbed and polished and put on exhibition at a Charleston museum, one issue remains:

Who actually discovered the resting place of the submarine for all those years after she went to the bottom of the sea following the attack on the *Housatonic*?

Was the discovery made by Clive Cussler's NUMA team as is officially proclaimed and generally believed?

Or was it Edward Lee Spence, who just happened on the submarine one day in 1970 when on a fishing trip in Charleston Harbor?

Much compelling evidence points to Spence as the actual discoverer, and Cussler must be accredited as the man who found (or refound) the submarine and brought it back to the light of day. Whatever Spence may say, unquestionably the *Hunley* would still lie below the seabed if Cussler's doggedness had not finally prevailed. Yet Spence's evidence is intriguing: His coordinates proved correct, or very nearly so. He still claims to be the original discoverer, and has masses of evidence to back it. But even if the adventure has now turned into an ego trip, for what it is worth he should be given official credit, even at this late date.

Meanwhile, the discoverers remain at legal odds. Politicians wrestle over the *Hunley*'s final resting and exhibit locale. Archaeologists ponder the source of the *Hunley*'s fate and the intricacies of her design, and marvel at the secrets to which she still clings. The voyage of the *Hunley* continues.

TIMELINE

SPRING 1863
Horace G. Hunley becomes one third shareholder of the
Singer Submarine Corps, an organization begun by engineer E. C. Singer to underwrite the cost of a third experi-
mental submarine, the first two having failed. Under the
direction of James McClintock and Lt. William A.
Alexander, the *H. L. Hunley* is built in Mobile.

JULY 31
The *Hunley* sinks a flatboat in a demonstration on the
Mobile River.

AUGUST 7
The *Hunley* is ordered by General Beauregard to
Charleston to combat the Union blockade of that port.

AUGUST 23
Upset by apparent failure of the *Hunley* crew to act, General Beauregard confiscates the submarine and mans it with a crew of Confederate navy volunteers. Lt. John Payne is in command.

AUGUST 29
The inexperienced crew causes the *Hunley* to submerge accidentally during a training exercise near Fort Johnson in Charleston Harbor. Five of the eight crew members drown. Two weeks later the *Hunley* is salvaged.

SEPTEMBER 19
Horace Hunley requests that the submarine be placed under his control and that he be allowed to furnish it with an experienced crew from Mobile.

OCTOBER 15
The *Hunley,* piloted by Captain Hunley, goes into an inadvertent dive during trials and sinks to the bottom of Charleston Harbor. All eight crew members, including Hunley, are drowned.

NOVEMBER 7
The *Hunley* is salvaged again. The bodies of Captain Hunley and his crew are buried in Magnolia Cemetery.

NOVEMBER 12

Lt George A. Dixon takes command of *Hunley.* The submarine is outfitted anew with volunteers from Mobile and the CSS *Indian Chief.*

1864
FEBRUARY 17

After several weeks of training the *Hunley* ventures forth to attack the U.S. steam frigate *Housatonic.* At 8:45 P.M. on a clear moonlit night the *Hunley* detonates a torpedo against the stern of the *Housatonic,* sinking her almost instantly. This is the first successful submarine attack on a warship in history. The *Hunley* heads back to her station but is lost on the way.

FEBRUARY 26

The U.S. Navy convenes a board of inquiry into the sinking of the *Housatonic.* The court absolves Captain Pickering of all blame, finding that the ship was "blown up and sunk by a rebel torpedo craft."

FEBRUARY 29

The sinking of the *Housatonic* is reported in the Charleston newspapers.

1865
The Civil War ends.

1870
OCTOBER 8
A Charleston newspaper reports (erroneously) that divers have found the wreck of the *Hunley* lying next to the sunken *Housatonic*. Speculation as to the fate of the submarine will continue for many years.

1909
FEBRUARY
The remaining wreckage of the *Housatonic* is dynamited, allowing navigation over the hull. Over the next few decades the ship's final resting place is covered with sand and forgotten.

1970
APRIL
Underwater explorer Edward Lee Spence discovers the *Hunley* by accident.

1980

Author Clive Cussler launches the first of several attempts to find the *Hunley.*

1995

Cussler announces the May 3, 1995, discovery of the *Hunley.*

SEPTEMBER 14

Edward Lee Spence donates his rights to *Hunley* to the state of South Carolina.

2000
AUGUST 8

The *Hunley* is raised and towed by barge to Charleston for conservation.

SEPTEMBER
Tours begin.

2001
Conservation continues.

INDEX